ALL GROWN UP

OVERLOOKED, UNDERVALUED AND UNDERESTIMATED

LEAH CHILENGWE

Commissioned Publication

A Commissioned Publication Printed by

MOORLEYS
Print, Design & Publishing
info@moorleys.co.uk · www.moorleys.co.uk

Dedication

To my friend, my confidant, my greatest cheerleader and husband Nelson, we did it! Thank you for always believing in me. You saw me even when I did not see myself.

To my girls Kookie and Zo, thank you for making it easy for me to look good as a mother. I honour your patience with me whilst juggling my life plates, I love you guys.

To my mother Betty Masengu, a woman with the biggest heart I have ever come across, you showed me the depths of a mother's love.

And last, but not least; if daddies were superheroes, you would be Superman! Ignatius Tom Daka Masengu, my daddy and my hero.

Contents

Acknowledgments

To all my family and friends, too numerous to mention by name. My eternal gratitude, for your support and encouragement. I could not have run this race without you cheering me on from the terraces!

My sister Kaluba Kahokola, I consider myself God's favourite for specifically and intricately slotting you into my life.

Thank you to Pastor Alex Phiri, for helping me edit this book. I broke many editing rules, but you supported me to find my voice and speak my words.

And to Angela and Tash thank you for teaching me love beyond my womb.

Introduction

Life has the amazing ability to teach us many lessons as it unfolds and progresses. While writing this book, I have realised, with greater clarity that the relationships that we develop, and the people we keep company with, are crucial to who we become.

Moreover, it does not matter, what level of education you may hold, nothing teaches us lessons as profound as these relationships we encounter.

The heart, as well as the soul, seems to know how to categorise the essential information stored for our well-being or otherwise. Deep down as the processing of that awareness takes place, we discover a *reluctance* to receive respectfully information, from the people who we feel are less important to us. Yet, by contrast, our family settings carry an authority to teach us lessons, whether we like it or not. The lessons that come from these relationships become the basis by which we fundamentally frame our lives.

In this book, I have touched on the way we, as humans, interact with people; with situations and the lessons, we draw from them.

The book originates largely from a personal experience, of exclusion, rejection, and hurt. My words aim to encourage readers facing similar circumstances and to help them understand their value.

I have also extensively alluded to Moses (in the bible) the deliverer of the Israelites from captivity. He too had similar experiences. I therefore, seek to draw out some parallels as well as lessons we too can take away from his journey.

All Grown up talks about how I overcame the challenges I faced in life, and it talks about how I am still learning to grow with the current ones. I know how audacious I may appear about some of the things I have spoken about in this volume. However, I am not, in any way, trying to, undermine, accuse, or blame those I have come across.

Everything we need to succeed in life has been already deposited within us. It is up to us to ensure that the negative experiences do not immobilise us because we were created to thrive. Your uniqueness is by design!

I hope and trust this book will be the key that unlocks your door to self-discovery, and to your true worth.

Chapter 1

ON YOUR MARKS...

I was born into a family of loving parents and privileged in a way that the western world does not appreciate or usually see on television broadcasts about Africa. Living in the western world however has been interesting, in that all too often I have felt it imperative to explain and enlighten numerous individuals concerning their inaccurate preconceived negative ideas about Africa. It is my belief that this ignorance is directly attributable to a lack of education, a misunderstanding and prejudice about the general wealth of the African continent with its many nations, and the scope and variety of its natural beauty. It has therefore been my observation that people's appreciation of anything in life is directly proportional to their knowledge or interest around it.

My early childhood recollection of my family was of parents who appeared very much in love. Both were educated people with ambition for their children. In retrospect, I can see how I have sought to model their relationship. My father was my *buddy*, I look back fondly to my relationship with him; he taught me to understand my value and worth that led to the unlocking of who I was called to be.

My family are passionate people, full of laughter and friendship. Much like the Italians, we love our food; enjoy family debates, as well as everyone speaking competitively at high decibel volume! I am the oldest of four children, originally five, but sadly, one sibling was 'promoted' to heaven at only two years of age.

Writing this book, has caused me to mentally 'park' for the longest period of my life, in the truth about the death of brother number two. When he fell ill, my mother was with him at the hospital for a while. When she eventually returned home, he was not with her; his passing was abrupt. To make matters worse, we never had an opportunity to say goodbye. At his funeral, the family thought that we were too young to face everything and decided that neither my siblings nor I should be part of the procession to put him to rest.

I remember life continuing as though nothing major had happened, although every mention of his name was in whispered tones. Now, as a mother myself, I have a greater appreciation of how difficult this time must have been for my mother. She must have been devastated. How could she not be? Looking at her now, I have the greatest wonder and admiration for her strength and dignity, and the way she continued with her duties as a wife and mother.

How remarkable is the power that remains in the face of losing so deeply, and yet still have the ability to soldier on?

It was a revelation, upon reflection, just how profoundly this particular event had affected me. I had another brother, not only two. Just because I could not see him physically, this did not mean he had not existed. He was a large part of who I am, and his departure had had a great impact; he mattered.

Daddy Dearest

My father was an intelligent man, full of wit and humour, a man of principles who lived his whole life loving his family. I have no doubt at all that he loved my siblings and I. One of my favourite characteristics of him was that he did not take himself too seriously. He believed in the simplicity of life and I admired his great desire to esteem others. There was also a *mischievous* side to him; he was not afraid to laugh at countless stories; about how certain behaviours in individuals tickled him. I refer to him in past tense because he has since passed away. I mention him specifically because he was pivotal in my journey to self-discovery. I have come to learn that many people have had similar experiences to me, and my experience and perspective is therefore just one of these stories.

One of my earliest memories is when I was around six or seven; I sensed that there was something not quite right with my family. What I was not aware of, was that my father had always had a mental illness and had already been diagnosed with Paranoid Schizophrenia.

Understanding the implications of this at such a tender age was far from easy. Looking back now, I realise this was one of my defining moments in the battle to discover who I really was meant to be. Admittedly, it is difficult to describe accurately what life was like, growing up. I struggled to cope with the internal battles and confusion that raged during my father's mental health relapses, yet in the main, I think I was reasonably happy.

On the other hand, I faced an internal battle to fight and control the anxiety that at times threatened to take me over, when the different aspects of my father's illness emerged. Initially, these episodes were occasional but as he grew older, they increased in occurrence. I understand now, how stressed I must have been, and how this situation contributed to me developing insecurities about myself as well as having a low self-image.

To top it all off, my father's relatives despised my mother. The very strength of most African cultures can at times be its greatest curse. Africans believe in community living, every older woman in the family is mum, every older man, dad. To this end, everyone somehow feels they have the permission and authority to voice opinions and issues directly into families even when it is not their place to do so.

Sometimes I felt we, my siblings and I, were fighting many wars on several fronts, along with the unspoken family dramas bubbling below the surface. For me, at a tender age, it was difficult to understand the family animosity.

Family should be our haven but most often, it is where we feel and endure our deepest pain.

My pain was fuelled by what I felt was unjustified behaviour from my father's relatives; they blamed my mother for dad's illness. This unfairness infuriated me. Their attitude also weighed heavily on me, like carrying a rucksack of rocks. To make matters worse, I felt powerless to do anything about it. I have come to understand that controlling other people's behaviour is an impossible mission. It took time, but eventually, I made a choice to turn a page on this pain and let it go. This was a huge relief; there was far more to life than remaining stuck in this place. I have since learnt the importance of not *'parking'* around the pain that is meant to propel us into our destiny.

The discovery that my father was ill and different became increasingly apparent. None of the other fathers I knew visited the 'special' hospital that became dad's temporary home when he had 'funny turns'. Faced with such life-changing experiences, it can often feel as though this is personally unique, but I have since realised that far more people than I imagined have faced similar crises with a loved one.

Sadly, it seems that people generally shun mental illness because it is a far less acceptable sickness in society, whereas other forms of illnesses like terminal illness are easier to manage in certain instances. Of course, there is still ignorance, prejudice, ill-disguised discomfort, careless statements and malicious gossip bandied around this particular health challenge, which causes unnecessary hurt for both the sufferer and family members. Despite my father's illness, he was an intelligent, educated man who provided and cared for us in ways more than most *'able minded'* fathers would, in caring for their own.

Even though I was young at the time, nobody told me to keep my dad's health problem a secret. I instinctively knew it was not something one could share with school friends in the playground or discuss at their dinner tables during sleepovers. Even so, it somehow became a known fact and a premise for gossip. My relationships changed, friends and acquaintances treated me differently as they learned of dad's illness – at least this is my perspective. My siblings have their own stories to tell. Coping with the change in my father was difficult, coupled with the tsunami of hatred spewing from my father's family. It is not easy to embrace who you are when the people who are supposed to be closest to you have rejected you. I became ashamed of this situation, which was not of my choosing, and the fear of judgement by a prejudiced society took hold.

For years, I existed in a state of fear. I accepted a label put on me because of dad's illness until it dawned on me that I was bigger than the label. By using my words wisely, I found my voice. I dared to stand up; I dared to speak out, and I dared to be different. My 'mountains' drove me higher, they taught me how to sing and *redefine* the music of my past. I would no longer blame family history for how I viewed myself. I had a future and as long as I refused to look through the rear-view mirror of life, I would be able to keep driving forward.

Every family has its fair share of drama; I have come to accept that. I guess the issues that a family faces should not influence how it is defined, it should rather be measured by its willingness to come together to work out the difficulties. To do this requires intimacy in relationships. A 'getting to know of each other' allows people to grow together consequently enabling an understanding of each other.

I learnt that because my family did not understand me, they could only strive to give me what was important to them at the expense of what was important to me.

When you grow up with dysfunction, you will sooner or later have to make choices to untangle the threads of family behaviours and belief systems in the search for your own truth. We can only figure out what the root of our problems is, and how to change things when we shine the light of clarity and reality on the situation.

In all these challenges however, the reality of it was that through my faith and trust in my God, He was there, with me. How do I know this fact? Because I have reached this point in my life, where I can write and share my heart.

Chapter 2

WHAT'S MY NAME?

I am known to be the inquisitive one in my family, my mother called it mischievousness, but I was not sure this was correct. I could see why she would say this though, because I am 'nosey' by nature. I am curious about people, curious about life, systems and culture, anything.

This character trait steered me to my love for *people watching*. I love to observe and learn about people, watching their habits and little idiosyncrasies, creating imaginary lives about them in my head. This characteristic also led me at a very young age to begin to wonder about who I was, and why it was that I existed. I was also curious about my temperament, and later understood my *'mischievous'* ways too. Mama was right; I now know I got my cheekiness from, my dad. He was a very funny man!

As child, I thought that if I could figure out the 'why' behind the way I was wired, I would have found the meaning to my life. The funny thing is this, I am still trying to work myself out, right up to this present time. This experience, therefore, led me to conclude that discovering who we are is a lifelong process. The questions I used to ask myself have remained the same, but the answers have changed significantly, over time.

Discovering the person that I was designed to be, has been exciting. Ultimately, it has become clear to me that the journey to understanding who I am, can only be concluded by answering a set of personal questions. I think that humans are self-searching beings, constantly living with the urge to evaluate ourselves. I tried to push the questions out of my mind, but I have since come to realise that they are a necessary part of a lifelong search, to understand ourselves, and our immediate surroundings.

I have come to realise through this journey, that self-discovery will stretch you. The stretching comes when you discover that there is a gap that requires navigating in order for you to actualise who you were called to be.

I have also discovered that this gap separates the persons that we are at any given time, and the persons that we were called to be. This is the reason why the journey across this gap can be stretching, as it is usually difficult to identify where we are on the gap spectrum when we face challenging issues.

My challenges have mostly arisen during times of personal crisis linked to my father's mental illness. There is something about *pain*, which causes one to begin to probe their identity.

I was also very clear, from a very young age that I disliked seeing other people treated unfairly. I preferred 'hanging around' the disadvantaged, rather than the so-called *privileged groups*. Even though I was generally liked growing up, I pushed so many boundaries, and certain quarters thought I was rebellious. I remember when I was in year eight taking a school report home that initially said; *"Leah is a good girl"*, but which the form teacher then amended to, *"Leah can be a good girl"*. My teacher had changed the report but had not even bothered to write it on a fresh piece of paper. I am not bitter or anything, but I have never forgotten this incident. I have since found the funny side of it. I was a girl with her own mind, from a very young age.

I have learnt now that what I called unfair at a young age is in fact prejudice. I despised, and a greater part of me still does – the marginalisation of people, regardless of who, or what they are! It is incredibly difficult for me to understand how it can ever be okay to reduce, negatively, a person's life chances, just because they do not fit a certain stereotype.

"Will you Pipe it Down!"

I was told I talked too much... I often heard the statement, *"Leah talks"!* There is nothing wrong with the statement itself I guess; however, the way it was said implied that my talking was a problem. I recall thinking the criticism was odd, as I could not understand why my talking was even an issue. I look back now, and realise that the more I heard, "Leah talks", the more it began to erode me.

It was this negative perception that begun the slow erosion of the aspects that were uniquely me. It led me to think that if my being too vocal was problematic to people, then maybe I really did have a problem. The more I spoke, the more the 'world' told me to sit down. Is it not funny how if you are not careful, you can let other people's problems become your own? We end up forgetting that we all have unique qualities and characteristics that distinguish us from other people

The problem with letting external voices influence your identity is that you begin to model yourself on individuals that you believe are accepted in society. At the core of who we are, there is 'something' that longs to adhere to a set of societal norms, because this gives us a sense of belonging.

Enter Mildred

I usually tell the story of a friend of mine, who I will call Mildred, for the purpose of this story. I have chosen this name probably because it is a perfectly good and a safe name to use, but also, because I do not personally know a Mildred.

I first met Mildred at kindergarten, and we did not see each other after that, until the first day, of the first year, at university. She walked up to me and asked if I remembered her being my best friend. What an impeccable memory! I really wanted to be like Mildred. Her memory, however, was not the only thing that I admired about her. I loved how sweet natured, soft-spoken and how kind hearted she was.

I wanted to be Mildred, not in a, *'I want your life kind of way'*, but rather being around her made me want to do better; she made me feel like I wanted to be better. Mildred also had no problems in the talking department like I was told I had. She was rather slow to speak and quick to listen. In my mind, Mildred was the type of person people seemed to find acceptable.

The problem with trying to *fit in* is that we can miss the key question, *"who am I"*? I wanted to change, so badly, that I ended up getting fixated with trying to slot into a mould that I now realise was never designed for me.

A lack of personal identity can make us shape ourselves into something, to fit into other people's expectations of who we should be. We, therefore, lose our authenticity trying to emulate a standard that has been artificially set for us. Take Mildred for instance, I wanted to be her so bad, but without any real understanding as to why she was introverted. Nothing in me really understood why she was the way she was, but I still modelled myself on her personality, and failed miserably! When we try to be something that we are not, we confuse ourselves and waste valuable growth opportunities in the process.

Recognising this fact, allowed me to understand that *everything* was created for a purpose and that I was born to fulfil a specific role in life. I was placed on this earth with a job description outlined for a specific assignment. Therefore, trying to be someone else meant that I was abdicating my duties. Besides, I could not do what I was meant to be doing, whilst chasing my tail trying to be Mildred.

It became increasingly clear to me that I was alive for a reason greater than I was, and far bigger than any paycheck or possessions, I held. The thing is this, when you live for a cause greater than yourself, possessions follow. Recognising that I had a divinely superior assignment led me to begin to seek it out.

The pursuit of trying to discover the 'Why' in my life's journey has been interesting. I have come to realise that most of us, have an awareness of purpose for our lives, and yet I have observed that instead of reaching out for it, we settle back, waiting for someone to pick us out for validation, and activate that purpose for us. For some unknown reason, we feel like we need validation from people in order to live authentically.

Waiting to be 'singled out' can lead to frustration because, what we are doing inadvertently, is putting our destiny into someone else's hands. We sit, and we wait to be selected, not sure by whom, but we wait anyway. In the end, we feel like time has run out and therefore, anxiety creeps in.

I used to be like that. I knew there was something in me that I was created for, and yet I hoped the people around me; the people I was connected to, those who I thought would recognise my potential, would give me a chance. I eventually realised that, in doing this, I had devolved the responsibility of living out my purpose, to someone else. I was letting the desire to be *picked,* outweigh the fact that I was already chosen; handpicked specifically for a journey that had been uniquely crafted for me.

The failure to recognise the importance of what we hold inside can make us devalue it. I learnt that it is near impossible to put a value on yourself when you lack self-belief. I began to believe in myself, *believe* that I could achieve results in spite of what other people thought of me.

The discovery of 'the gap' between who certain people thought I was, and who I really was, was a huge revelation in my journey. The space that existed between where I was at the time and where I was heading to was a huge determinant of my value. You see, if you treat yourself as *second class* you will never appreciate your real potential. It is in appreciating what you carry that you find your true value.

Letting someone else put a price tag on your potential will significantly reduce your worth and result in you being underappreciated. How people treat us most times, lies in how we treat ourselves. We teach other people how we want to be treated. This is because we cannot 'sell' our worth to others, until we see it for ourselves first.

I have learnt that it is illogical to put your destiny, crafted in heaven's throne room, into the hands of an earthly being, who was not even present at your creation. On your journey to your life's mission do not let, *"picked"*, become the obstacle to, *"chosen"*. You cannot let the fact that the people you thought mattered, did not choose you, to define who you are. There are approximately seven billion people on planet earth. This means that there are many options out there believe me.

For me, the freedom to express who I was created to be, came when I recognised that just because some people did not like my talking; it did not mean that being vocal was not useful in the grand scheme of my life's assignment. In the end, I came full circle; the very thing for which they criticised me growing up, is what I have discovered was specifically designed to be used to help others, in my own way.

People will have opinions about who they think you should be; life has shown me this. They may even overlook, undervalue, and underestimate you, but you cannot let that deter you. You need to recognise that everyone has their story, it is therefore, your job to understand that maybe you were never meant to be part of their cast. You *must* feel okay about this fact in order to 'grow'.

We very often lose valuable time trying to convince people that we can be an asset to their circle. We scream on the inside, "Use me"! But, we have to remember that we cannot control what people say, or do to us, we can only govern how we react. To ensure that we protect our God-given identity; it is our job not to let outside influences to get to inside of us.

Not knowing who I was, made it difficult for me to deal with what I saw as being snubbed by the 'circles' I so desperately wanted to belong to. I found myself vacillating between who I knew I was and who, I had come to understand, *they* wanted me to be. I call this the *'pendulum effect'*. The pendulum effect exhausts energy, it has no end destination, and it only oscillates between two points therefore hindering your progress to any meaningful goal. I accept, and reluctantly acknowledge that some people will not like certain things about me, and it will be difficult to establish any concrete reasons as to why they feel the way they do. However, the more I discover who I am, and my principal mission in life, the more I have found it easy to deal with what I saw, and in some cases still see, I guess, as their rejection.

What's Good God?

The greatest relationship that I have found – my faith in God – has helped me to understand who I am. There is a story in the bible about a guy called Moses. God told Moses that he had seen the oppression of his people, the Israelites, in Egypt. And He said he had heard their cries of distress because of the ill- treatment from their slave masters. As a result, God wanted Moses to go and save the Israelites from this cruelty!

For this reason, I have come to know that whenever God has something that He needs doing, He always handpicks someone for the job. We read in Exodus 4:10 (NLT):

> "But Moses pleaded with the Lord, "O Lord, I'm not very good with words. I never have been, and I'm not now, even though you have spoken to me. I get tongue-tied, and my words get tangled".

Moses in this situation protested because he believed that he was not good enough for this task. In his mind, his lack of eloquence in his speech disqualified him from the job at hand. However, God's response to Moses, in verse 11, is mind blowing:

> "Then the Lord asked Moses, who makes a person's mouth? Who decides whether people speak or do not speak, hear or do not hear, see or do not see? Is it not I, the Lord? Now go! I will be with you as you speak, and I will instruct you in what to say".

Moses felt inadequate. He, without doubt, thought he was not fit for the role; in fact, he may have felt that he did not look the part. According to him, there were better orators among the Israelites that God could have chosen. Besides, Moses may have been intimidated by the fact that some of his own people had already rejected him after he had killed an Egyptian (see Exodus 2). In short, Moses felt that he did not have what it took to be a leader and God's mouthpiece!

19

In reading the above passages, I began to realise that Moses' journey was much more like mine, in more ways than I had first realised. I can easily relate to Moses feelings of inadequacy in my *self-exploration* journey. For Moses, I love the fact that God encouraged him.

God was like, "yes, go on and speak to Pharaoh, stutter and stammer your way through because guess what? I will be right there to tell you what you should say".

God is very specific in his purposes and deliberate about who He chooses to fulfil His plans through. Because of this, I believe that everyone was intentionally crafted, and explicitly set out for a specific calling in life. I know for a fact that I am the way I am because God wants me to get a certain job done, before I vacate this earth.

My focus now has changed. I have stopped chasing what certain quarters consider acceptable. Instead, I concentrate on searching out the real reason for my existence. Trying to *fit in...* is so much harder than finding *your fit*. My fit is that aspect that comes easy to me, but which others find surprisingly hard to do, the very thing whose value I had been questioning. To try to *'fit in'* will require you to alter your *fit*, the very aspect that was crafted uniquely for you to fulfil your purpose.

When I look back now, I realise I could not change who I was even if I tried. My character was rooted in my DNA; it was who I was. It did not matter how much I tried to be demure it was just not me. I was not 'wired' that way! No matter how hard I tried, if I had something to say, it would come out, one way or the other! Besides, I am very convinced that it is difficult to fit into the definition of what is considered normal in another person's head.

I understand now that the parts of my life where I wanted to be like Mildred were in fact the areas where I was already perfect for the journey that was carved out for me. This meant that I just needed to embrace me, to enjoy the person that I was created to be. Pretending to be someone else is a waste of who you are. This has helped me to grow more, and to fill the big shoes I was created to fill – my own shoes for that matter, not another person's.

Finding out who you were called to be, with or without the approval of others will catapult you to the level that you were designed to be. The thing is this, we are all on a journey; we are all going through a process. It is important not to let our circumstances define who, and how we should be. Our strength lies in maintaining our uniqueness. We should not to give up on who we are, in favour of who *'they'* think we should be. I came to the realisation that the blessing was on who I was, and not who *they* thought I ought to be.

As for Mildred, she is still my friend, turned sister, in case you are wondering. I did not murder her and steal her life. Together, our lives are richer for the diversity we share in our relationship, and oh, did I say that she was '*hot*'?

Chapter 3

ARE YOU BREAKING UP WITH ME?

I may have been nine or ten when I experienced a *traumatic* friendship breakup, in a way that only a nine-year-old can.

I used to have a best friend; I loved this girl with all my heart. We had been friends since first grade. Being a girl of that age, one of your biggest ambitions is to get a *'best friend'*. I had one; I had made it, or so I thought! We went to each other's homes for play dates, sleepovers, and spent most of our time together.

One day out of the blue, I walked into class and this *kid* had written me a three page, A4 lined, "*Dear John*" letter. I look back now and ask myself,

"*What was that*"? Where does a nine-year-old get the commitment to put *meanness* to paper covering three whole pages? The letter I was handed outlined every element about me that she did not like. To be honest, I too felt "*a certain way*", about some things concerning her, but I did not have the commitment to write her a three-paged A4 letter!

She walked up to me with a smile, which I now suspect might have been a sneer or even a cross between a sinister look and a smirk! She handed me this pamphlet of a letter, to read. We had not fallen out or anything. In fact, she had been at my house only the weekend before she '*broke up*' with me. I was shaking and fighting to hold back my tears, whilst I tried to read the letter. I remember her laughing and asking me what I thought about it.

My *little* world had crumbled around me. I was hurt, confused and shocked, all wrapped in one. This was supposed to be my best friend. I later found out that she had written this *mean letter* with the assistance from her brother and his friends. I look back now and understand this to be just kids being good at what they do. It did not make what happened okay, but I now understand it from a mature perspective.

I have been blessed with wonderful friends since, but for me, this incident remained etched in my memory and became one of the main filters through which I developed most relationships in my later years. I let this letter's limited description of who she thought I was, define me.

It is funny how something like this can make you change who you are, to fit into what they have said about you? In the end, you accept a redefinition of who you are!

I will never really know what turned her heart against me, but what I know, looking back is that she was dedicated to ending our friendship. When one is committed to ending a relationship, there is nothing you can do about it. You cannot force someone to love you, and you certainly cannot go about trying to mould yourself into who '*they*' think you ought to be, in order to be accepted. Imagine the enormous task we would have on our hands if *life* called for us to amend who we were, based on people's description of who we were meant to be?

'Calcification'

A calcified heart is difficult to touch. It has layers that have piled on top of it from years of hurt, making it difficult to get to it. This incidence for me was a contributor to the gradual calcification of my heart. When your heart calcifies it inadvertently causes you to rely on yourself for protection from hurt. I realise now, that the thing I had built to protect me, had now become a labyrinth that would set out to destroy me if I was not careful.

Because of this, I became *'strong'*. Although I demonstrated strength of character, I was actually sensitive, insecure and full of self-doubt when it came to people and relationships. My *perceived* strength was such a strong force in my personality, but it was only a shield to protect myself from the world.

Vulnerability was the enemy as far as I was concerned. In my reasoning, if I behaved as though I was strong, then people would not think that I was a *walk over*. This was far from the truth because the fact is that vulnerability does not translate weakness or submissiveness to other people's ideologies.

To the contrary, it implies the courage to be yourself. This means replacing the 'strong' persona with the acceptance of what we need to change about ourselves. To show vulnerability is to show one's strength, the strength of character and determination to overcome. I have since learnt that in my world, being vulnerable is a bridge that develops healthy relationships.

The *"Dear John"* letter I mentioned previously was the earliest memory of what I now see as the introduction of rejection in my life, by people outside my family. And as I grew older, it would come in different forms and in different waves. My response to rejection, however, has evolved with each relationship incidence and challenge I have faced.

When people say they no longer want to be around us, we can easily take that as an accusation of some sort. What this statement says to us is, *"you are not good enough to be in a certain space"*. However, what we forget is that this statement is merely relevant to a *specific sphere*. When people reject us, there is the danger that we can take the incident as a testament to feeling like the whole world is rejecting us. However, this is not so and is only limited to a particular interaction.

The lie that comes with not being liked makes *'exclusion'* to become a blanket statement for everything, and everyone in our world. I think that if we recognised this accusation for what it is, and ring-fenced it, we would free ourselves from trying to convince everyone that we are good enough.

The *"Dear John syndrome"* can follow you in life, and it evolves as you evolve, morphing into differing forms. All of us have experienced this. You cannot be alive today without being sidelined, one way, or the other. What we need to learn, however, is how we navigate this. Setting new standards for ourselves starts in our thinking. Besides, nothing changes until we refuse to accept other people's limited view of us.

Remember the story of Moses? He was born to an Israelite woman when the reigning Pharaoh had made a decree to kill all the Hebrew male children at birth. Moses' mum, however, devised a plan to hide him, to save her son.

The background to this story is that after the death of Joseph, the Israelites multiplied greatly, became fruitful, and grew exceedingly strong to the extent that the land was full of them. Then a new Pharaoh who did not know Joseph took over Egypt. He became fearful of the Israelites, knowing that they had become too many. And so, Pharaoh dealt shrewdly with the Hebrews, for fear that they would turn against his Kingdom. He then proceeded to set taskmasters over them, to afflict God's people with heavy burdens.

So, Moses grew up in this environment, a setting in which he may have felt like he did not belong. Moses may have tried to 'fit in'. He may have attempted to conform to the traditions of his adopted people. Thinking of this made me recount similar occasions where I felt like I too, did not belong no matter how much I tried to conform to the *practices* of 'a place'.

I have at times, felt *too black* to be in the '*white world*' and oddly enough, sometimes, '*too white*' to fully integrate into my own society. I was constantly trying to prove my worth to some people, at different stages of my life! I learnt during this time that if you find yourself constantly trying to prove your worth, then there is a strong possibility that you have already forgotten your value.

When you dread people's disapproval, pleasing them becomes the easier option. And so, you fail to speak up, and you fail to express who you really are on the inside. It is easier to hear *'their'* words of approval than to face *disapproval from 'them'*.

Moses too may have experienced this tension of trying to act in ways to make himself accepted. He was not an Egyptian, but his mannerisms might have been as though he were one. Eventually, and whilst living in Pharaoh's palace, Moses killed an Egyptian he had seen beating one of the Hebrew slaves.

In Exodus 2:11-15, we read this about Moses:

> "Many years later, when Moses had grown up, he went out to visit his own people, the Hebrews, and he saw how hard they were forced to work. During his visit, he saw an Egyptian beating one of his fellow Hebrews. 12 After looking in all directions to make sure no one was watching, Moses killed the Egyptian and hid the body in the sand".

Wait a minute, you may ask, was Moses not an Egyptian? Did he not have any loyalty to the Egyptians who had raised him? It would seem to me though that by this act, Moses was making the decision to identify himself with the *'slave'*, in the field, and not the *'prince'*, in the palace.

Two things stand out for me, from this passage. It says that Moses looked and saw his "brothers", all of them in *forced* hard labour. *He saw his brothers*? When did it dawn on Moses that the Israelites were his brothers? What had happened to this prince that made him feel that he now belonged in the field? What was life like growing up among Egyptians as a royal when they knew he was a descendant of the slaves? Did he feel rejected? Was he marginalised? Was he sidelined in the Egyptian camp? Even though this may not be explicit in the scriptures, I believe that this position is not only implied, but I also do not believe that Moses woke up one day and decided he would kill an Egyptian.

It must have come through a long and hard process of reflection. Moses must have had a hard time vacillating between being a Hebrew, and an Egyptian, up to the point that *He cracked*. I believe that this must have been the beginning of his journey to self-discovery.

Who Decides…?

As I said earlier, the desire to belong is at the core of who we are as humans. It is our duty to make sure, however, that this desire does not outweigh our own self-worth. We need to awaken to the fact that we are valued and loved by one whose power is far greater than the validation of other people. In other words, we cannot lose ourselves to the desire to be accepted.

Look at Moses, on the surface; we may think that he had all the *trappings* of wealth and comfort living in the palace. *He surely did not need to rock the boat; he was privileged.* However, having discovered who he was, nothing was ever going to keep him from the *fields*. To him, he was an Israelite and no amount of wealth, position or power, would keep him away from that.

I too for the longest time wanted acceptance, I wanted to fit in, and I guess to an extent, I still do. And I have now come to accept that this is a natural desire in us human beings. The need to be accepted is not in itself wrong; the key, however, is how it is managed. You must ensure that this quest does not drive you, because when it *takes over,* there is a danger of losing yourself.

I have tried to be like other people in my life's journey. I copied other people because I thought I would gain acceptance. So, if we cannot accept ourselves as we really are, how can we expect other people to?

Not everyone is going to like us and to be honest we will not like everyone ourselves. Every encounter is, therefore, a blessing to us and we should never pass on the opportunity to grow from our experiences.

The change in attitude for me did not come overnight! I had to go through a rough process. I had to face a lot more *shuns and chops* from people, before I got to this *carefree stage in my life!*

My nine-year-old bestie and I never spoke again after she handed me that letter. However, in the days following the letter incident, I tried hard to practise who I thought she wanted me to be, in the hope that she would recognise the friend in me that she had desired. That day never came. She died a few years later when we were still teenagers. For me, she died too early to fix anything I thought had broken between us. *It was way too early for me!*

I learnt that you must accept at times, that no matter how much you try to change yourself, it will never be enough to please some people. You have to make peace with the fact that, if they were meant to be in your life they would accept the 'whole' of you; warts and all!

What kind of people, circumstances, or sounds, remind you that you were rejected; that people dropped and discarded you? What painful memories come to mind when you encounter the words such as neglected, overlooked, ignored, dismissed and betrayed? *So, they left, they did not choose you, and they ignored you, but so what?*

A lot happens in life that has the potential to *cripple and distort* who you are as a person, if you let it!

The people that hurt us the most are the ones in our inner circles, the ones we trust, the ones we feel should know better!

In my life, I have learned that some people will voice their thoughts with such *'volume and strength'* that we end up forgetting that they are merely airing their opinions! Do not let another person's view of you undermine your authentic value. Be willing to choose a different reality.

With the benefit of hindsight, I look at some moments in my life, and say *"so what"*? I now wish I had understood then, the *SO WHATS,* in those moments. I wish now, that at that time, I had the wherewith to interpret those situations as evidence of someone's perception of me, rather than as evidence and a consequent finality of my *'flawed'* nature.

So, I have come to accept that I will get marginalised now and then and I cannot do anything about that. What is within my power to control, is the ability to work on getting over it; to focus on the *'me'* that many others have accepted, and to surround myself with people that allow me to grow, without having the thoughts to discard me, when they think that I am imperfect.

Being aware of the unpleasant experiences is one thing, focusing on them is another. Do not feed that *experience* by giving it too much attention.

Focusing on it gives it too much control over you so, *do not give it power*!

The feeling of not being good enough is subjective, but it can be an opportunity for learning and growth. I have learnt to use these types of experiences as an opportunity to contemplate my current behaviours, and determine ways to grow, and become a better person.

So, if they walk away, then they were never meant to stay because those who were meant to stay will never leave!

Chapter 4

WHY CAN'T THEY SEE ME?

My intention in writing this book was to put my thoughts in print for posterity to look up. The process of writing this book has been cathartic for me. It has made me evaluate things, to let go of some hurts, and it has also enabled me to begin to redefine my thinking around who I thought I was. This process made me *lean back* into my life; to explore the interactions I have had with the different people I have come across on my journey. In doing so, I ended up concluding that as humans, we are conceivably a sum total of our life experiences.

As my life progressed, it became clear that there was a pattern linked to how I was reacting to the events I encountered. I was dancing to a rhythm in life that was dictated by the whispers in my heart connected to my past. We must never underestimate the impact of the things we have been through, or words that were spoken over us. It became clear to me, that the events I had encountered, positive, or negative, had a way of reshaping the person I would become. None of us is the same as we were yesterday, nor will be the same tomorrow.

I have repeatedly spoken about Moses in this book because I am fascinated by his story and the parallels I see with my own life. For me, over time, some of the stories I had heard about Moses appeared to have been simplified. Far from being an advocate for complexity, I believe that in the quest of telling a quick story, some Sunday school settings may have liquidated a deeper version of Moses' journey. Because of this interest, I stepped into the Scriptures to explore how life in the palace may have shaped Moses. For example, in Exodus 1:10, we read:

> A new king came to power in Egypt who didn't know Joseph. He spoke to his people in alarm, "There are way too many of these Israelites for us to handle. We've got to do something: Let's devise a plan to contain them, lest if there's a war they should join our enemies, or just walk off and leave us".

This passage seems to indicate that Moses was born into a hostile world. He was raised in a superpower of a nation, to an oppressed race, and during a time when all the male Israelite babies were under a royal death sentence. Remember Pharaoh had devised a plan to oppress the Hebrews, because they were way too many for the Egyptians to handle. So, the Pharaoh made a decree that when Jewish women went into labour, the Egyptian midwives were to inspect the baby's gender and to kill it, if it was a boy. *What was this guy smoking?*

What possesses a man to wake up and devise a strategy to reduce a whole nation's chances at success, all because he had built up an irrational fear of them?

Unfortunately (or is it, fortunately, depending on which perspective you are looking at), the more God's people were afflicted, the more they multiplied and grew stronger. The Israelites increase in numbers led to the people of Egypt to dread them even more and thus made their lives bitter.

Moses, nevertheless, had something special in his favour. The bible records in Hebrews 11:23:

'By faith Moses, when he was born, was hidden three months by his parents and were not afraid of breaking the king's demand'.

But, when his mother could no longer hide him, she put him in a basket and laid it in the reeds by the river bank. When Pharaoh's daughter came down to the river, she saw the basket floating among the reeds. To cut a long story short, she adopted Moses and he lived in the palace with her.

The Palace

Being the adopted son of Pharaoh's daughter meant that Moses was part of the royal family. In one of his writings, the ancient Jewish historian Josephus articulates that Moses could have been a potential heir to the throne and that as a young man he led the Pharaoh's armies in a victorious battle against the Ethiopians. He was raised with both, the science and learning of Egypt, an education that would not have been accessible to his native people.

Egypt was one of the most academic and scientific societies on the earth at that time. Since he was part of the royal family, I imagine that Moses was transported in a chariot fit for a Prince as he went about his business. I also used to think, that as a baby he entered the palace after being weaned, but according to Jewish rabbinical traditions, weaning could take place anywhere between eighteen months and five years of age.

No specific age is given for when Moses was weaned, but the weaning is mentioned. It is likely that he was between two and five years old when he moved to the palace. This to me suggests that his mother may have had a bigger influence on his life, than the oversimplified narrative I had encountered previously. Moses' formative years were most certainly influenced by his mother's heritage.

Historians also think that at the time Moses was adopted, the Egyptians were famous - or – infamous for their proud sense of racial superiority towards all other races. They maintained a substantial sense of ethnic pride that caused them to consider foreigners as inferior.

I am therefore not surprised that they were afraid and therefore marginalising this strong minority group in their midst. Given this history and that, Moses was an Israelite; it gives me clearer insight as to what Moses' experience may have really been like in the palace. Egypt had such an entrenched system of *apartheid* that there was potential for the Hebrews to grow over several centuries, without being assimilated in the Egyptian system.

As such, I find it difficult to believe that Moses was raised in this environment and yet had not encountered some kind of confusion about his identity. He must have grown up knowing what the people around him really thought of his kind.

Moses' story is a story of countless people worldwide, where for a variety of reasons, oppressive strategies, are implemented against certain groups. When people judge you as unworthy, you begin to act like it. But, it is your job to get a hold of yourself because you cannot do what you were called to do, whilst judging yourself as undeserving. It is our responsibility, all of us as citizens of the world, to be able to put ourselves in other people's shoes and see the big and accurate perspective of their experiences.

I have heard statements from even respectable people who say that biases are part of life because we all have them. This is true to an extent. However, is it not funny that the people that use this as an excuse or *mantra* are usually the ones who probably have never felt any form of systematic oppression? I find this whole argument to be flawed, weak and probably used as an avoidance to look at the issues staring us in the face, every day.

It is disappointing to see that time and time again; some people refuse to see injustices against other people for the sole purpose of protecting personal positions. Even Pharaoh was like that, the perpetuation of systemic oppression against the Israelites, in his mind, at least, ensured a protected position of his leadership.

The ability to step out of where we are and try to understand, objectively, the pain of another person, demonstrates true love for a 'brother'. I have learnt that just because it is not happening to me, it does not necessarily mean, *'it is not happening'*.

Imagine with me if you will; the Israelites complaining about being ill-treated, imagine them campaigning for equality, access to fair education for their children, and fighting for humane treatment. Without doubt, the Hebrews too may have had some form of bias towards the Egyptians. Who would not develop their own prejudices, if they were being oppressed? The main difference between these two people groups, however, is that the Israelites were not in authority, in these circumstances.

When you do not have power, your bias is pointless, in my view. You cannot affect anyone when you do not have the upper hand. Given that power is everything, it determines how people get affected when you hold a prejudgement. I used to get angry about this, but not anymore, because I realised that just because the Israelites were oppressed it did not take away from who they were. They were still a *chosen* people.

In my formative years, I formulated a narrative that resulted in me feeling like I was falling short of societal standards. I felt like I was an outsider. If rejection is all you have ever known all your life, it is easy to move from one oppressive system to the next and not be aware of it. You attract, to yourself, who you are on the inside. I saw this in my choice of friends, the men I dated, in my work, and generally most of all the other people I interacted with.

I have come to realise that the world can smell a *walkover* when it sees one. It is as if the label is on the forehead, and flashing, '*I am here, come and get me!*'

This was a pattern I found difficult to escape. Most times, I did not even know I was doing it. I was walking through life asking for people's permission to just be the person I was created to be. In response to this, I developed a hard exterior as a mechanism to protect what I knew to be delicate on the inside of me. The sad thing with situations like these is that we then end up dealing with a constant internal struggle. Because we know the truth about who we are, we look at the world, and how hard it is to be accepted, then begin to live with the question, '*why can't they see me*'? The origins of this question originates from a a deep internal struggle.

Can They not See?

'*Why can they not see?*' This question for me is a *job application*, an application for a job that you do not even want. You end up in a profession you have now applied for, that places a demand on you, to prove that you are worthy, that you are good enough. What happens then, is that you then work harder than everyone else works. You end up doing jobs others will not do and bite your tongue even when you know someone has literally wiped his or her feet all over your face, just to show that you are committed to *them*!

Eventually, you get so frustrated that you begin to hit back. You get angry, and lash out because you realise, I applied for a job I did not even ask for; working for a system that does not even want me, and there is no tangible return to show for it. From these outbursts of anger and lashing out, you begin to appear dysfunctional, and so you *play nicely* into a system that will label you as having a *'chip on your shoulder'*. When you get to this stage, you realise that you have, well and truly, given your power away, and it becomes necessary to walk through that *'open door'* and slam it behind you!

I have also come to learn that trying to convince people about who I am is a waste of valuable time and investments I could be making towards my future. I believe that the people who are called to *journey* with you will see your value. If they do not see it, *'don't sweat it'*, God will always send someone else.

In Moses' case, the Israelites could have tried to assure the Egyptians regarding their irrational fears. They could have worked until their fingers fell off, done all the training that was required, volunteered for extra manual work! But, until the latter became willing to lay down their worries, it was impossible for them to hear things from the children of Israel's point of view. Therefore, until we are willing to *'walk round the table'*, and to stand where other people are, we will never be able to see things from their point of view.

'The Fro'

I have a funny story about an incident involving my afro, which I fondly refer to as my 'fro'. I suppose the story would have been a sad one if it were not funny.

Some years back, I was working for a certain organisation. One specific incident stands out for me. One morning, I was preparing to lead a meeting with some *big shots*, and I was feeling pretty good about myself because I was confident in what I was about to deliver. I was eager to impress the audience; I figured this was my moment to *shine*. The internal dialogue went a little like this, *"if I just show them how brilliantly I can do this, they will see me, I mean really see me"!* My desire to be recognised for who I was became an obsession. I believed somehow that their validation would rub off years of the *pain*.

I turned up to this meeting dressed in my power suit and stilettos (my love for heels is another matter for another conversation). Way before my time in this organisation, I had made the decision to quit putting chemicals in my hair in order to straighten my natural curls. I had let go of the Eurocentric ideal of what is described as beautiful and learnt to love my natural curls!

Anyway, I am at this meeting, and this is now two years into my *'natural hair'* journey, feeling unbelievably free. As a side note, it amazes me when I read articles in some quarters about how for a woman of colour to walk around with natural curls is considered 'militant'. How does the hair God gave me, suddenly become a political crusade? When questions like these come to my mind, I remember Pharaoh's irrational fear, I take a step back and relax because I realise that the issue is more about them, than it is about me.

Back to my meeting: A very influential guy I had met regularly in these settings asked for a *quick word* before we started. I followed him outside where he started his sentence with, *"don't take this the wrong way..."* I should have stopped him at that point, because every time someone chooses to prefix what they are going to say with a statement like the one above, be prepared to be insulted!

I was not, in the least, prepared for the level of ignorance that came out of the mouth of one holding such a senior position in that organisation, as this man was. He asked me if I had considered straightening my hair, to "soften" my image, as my appearance could be considered "aggressive" in some circles. I think he may have noticed the puzzled look on my face when he gestured with his head towards mine and preceded to whisper, 'I think it will help the others out'.

To cut a long story short, I kept turning up to those meetings with my natural curls! I reckoned that if I could handle sitting with him for hours on end, in his sweaty, ill-fitting suits, and sometimes in poorly conditioned rooms, he surely could live with my hair!

The point I am trying to make is that it is not our differences that divide us, it is our inability to recognise, accept and celebrate variability. I believe that reacting negatively to something just because it does not feel familiar is to have a very narrow view of the beautiful diversity that we live in.

My faith has been my anchor in my journey, without it, I think I would have probably *gone crazy* by now.

Proverbs 4:7 instructs us to, *"get wisdom and to get understanding"*.

If Pharaoh had a bit of wisdom and understanding, he would have had better insight, and the Israelites would have gotten better treatment under his reign. I have come to find peace, however, in that, I now understand that regardless of what Pharaoh thought or said about the Children of Israel, this did not take away from their identity.

So, my statement in life is, *"I am chosen."* This is not to try to convince anyone; it is rather a reinforcement to myself that I really am. I belong *'here'*, a place specifically carved out for me, with space enough for my Afro! Besides, the way we see ourselves will have an impact on how we treat others and vice versa.

Hurting people is not only done by *'villains,'* we all do it, one way or another. We have an impact on people in more ways than we can ever understand. I read something once that I have come to love, and it reads as follows: *"Sometimes I feel discriminated against, but it does not make me mad any more. I am merely astonished that they deny themselves the pleasure of my company"*. For me, embracing this statement helped me *find* myself.

You can sometimes look back at some past relationships, the jobs you have held on to, the habits you tolerated, the behaviours you allowed, and think, *"what a waste"!* However, my belief is that, nothing in life is ever wasted for it leaves a deposit inside you, that you can use.

Chapter 5

A TIME TO KILL

Thereere comes a time, after all has been said and done, and regardless of the experiences of the past, when you need to decide the path you will take, to free yourself from the shackles of bygone hurts. Your current environment should not affect your ability to live out your full potential.

Remember, your decisions often reflect who you are. Therefore, it is important to find your true self, before you decide you want some adjustments to your life. No positive changes will take place in your life if you wait for someone else to help you. Be responsible for your own personal transformation. The resolve to overcoming life's hurdles begins and ends in the mind. Personal development, especially when you have grown up being told, or made to feel that you are not good enough, calls for a paradigm shift!

We should always be open to the fact that everything has a beginning and an end, therefore, change is inevitable. In fact, it is hard to know how deeply entrenched some of the past hurts in your life are, until you embark on a journey to self-discovery.

Unresolved hurts can go undetected for a long time, and all the while damaging you from the inside, like a cancer. The things people have said and done let alone your own negative thoughts; all can lie festering for ages just waiting for the right conditions to cause them to bubble over.

Moses was 40 years old when he snapped, emotionally. We read in Hebrews 11:24, 25:

> "It was by faith that Moses, when he grew up, refused to be called the son of Pharaoh's daughter. He chose to share the oppression of God's people instead of enjoying the fleeting pleasures of sin".

Killing the Egyptian

Moses was all grown up! Obviously, his internal conflict was a result of the oppression at the hands of the Egyptians, and to a certain degree, his own people! Acts 7: 23-25 describes Moses' actions at

40 years old, to avenge his 'brothers' mistreatment. What took him so long?

> One day when Moses was forty years old, he decided to visit his relatives, the people of Israel. He saw an Egyptian mistreating an Israelite.
>
> So, Moses came to the man's defense and avenged him, killing the Egyptian. Moses assumed his fellow Israelites would realize that God had sent him to rescue them, but they didn't.

Clearly, Moses was battling an internal conflict of identity. What was an *'Egyptian'* doing killing another Egyptian? should they not have been on the same side? Moses may have been having an identity crisis; he was too Hebrew to be Egyptian, and too Egyptian to be Hebrew. Besides, his name, Moses, and the backdrop of his adoption as the Son of Pharaoh's daughter, must have been too much for any Hebrew to ignore. No doubt, his fellow Israelites were uncomfortable with his 'double ancestry', if we go by the scripture we just read, above.

Moses' inner battles and palace experiences must have brought him to the point that he committed murder. Clearly, Moses did not leave the palace that day with murder on his mind. He simply reacted to an act of injustice. He snapped on the inside when he saw an Egyptian mistreating one of his own people.

What Moses witnessed that day must have set off a series of negative memories in him – vivid recollections of some of the events in his own past. In the Message bible, in Exodus 2:11-15, we read this about Moses' next course of action after committing murder.

> He looked this way and then that; when he realized there was no one in sight, he killed the Egyptian and buried him in the sand.

Like Moses, we can all have default settings that condition how we respond every time we feel that someone has intruded into the areas of our emotional injuries.

Without knowing it, all of us have negative beliefs about ourselves that we feel quite devastated about. These destructive thought patterns can take us down an unbearable dark hole of emotional pain, and even make us hurt the people around us, if left unchecked.

Very few people understand how stressful it is to try to explain the battles that go on in one's head (and sometimes the heart) especially when you, the person at the centre of the internal conflict, cannot fully understand what is happening, in the first place.

The voices from the past tend to follow us – repeating all our past hurts, insecurities and anxieties. Eventually, the loudest voice tends to build a stronghold – the mask that the people around us start to see.

Afterwards, most people in these types of situations may start to develop certain phobias about the future, when in fact it is their past – the repeated core negative beliefs, that paralyse their current and future creativity.

Thus 'Killing the Egyptian' in the context of this book is not about actual murder, but rather a figure of speech aimed at encouraging us to free ourselves from the grip of the oppression that has caused us to embrace a false self, for most of our lives.

Similarly, it is near impossible to reach for your destiny whilst still tied to the past. It is like driving a car and looking in the rear view mirror. The result will be catastrophic! Break away from anything that wants to keep you anchored to a fractured past; it is a progress stealer!

Rehashing emotional wounds, especially those caused by harmful words and actions, towards us, will weigh us down and stifle our hunger for a better tomorrow.

My belief is that, your reaction to the events that caused you pain, is a story in itself, and there is no need to feel ashamed about it. Depending on the response, it may indicate that something needs adjusting on the inside. Free yourself from the prison of your past and change your story if you must! That very act of confronting the traumas in your life is what I have referred to as, *'killing the Egyptian'*.

Slaying the Egyptian in one's life, calls for a lot of self-introspection. The inward look will help you to find those areas of brokenness, the negative self-beliefs, the torture from the insensitive words of those in *authority* over you. A deep inner search may also help to identify what triggers your reactions to some specific events of your life.

Sometimes, to recover our sense of significance and relevance, we need to separate ourselves from the people responsible for the internal conflicts that have made us have a lop-sided view of the gift that life is. This means creating boundaries – rules that *you say* cannot be broken without consequence. For example, below are some boundaries I have set for myself after I decided I was not going to let anything stop me from reaching for my purpose. I want to share these principles with you.

'See No Evil'

Never take the choice of separating one's self from vitriolic people as an *'unforgiveness'*. I struggled with this notion in the past, until I arrived at the conclusion that this kind of separation is just one of the first steps to freedom. This also means that you recognise at some point that perhaps the person that God designed you to be, cannot fit certain social circles. With this thought in mind, tell the toxic people in your life: "God bless you, be happy but, I will not read your mail or see you, if your presence continues to perpetuate the pain in my life".

'Hear No Evil'

Stop listening to people who continuously inject you with verbal venom. Their diatribes will without doubt sabotage your spiritual, emotional and physical wellbeing.

In fact, I am always wary of "friends" who tell me the awful things that other people say about me. When that happens I am like, *"child, keep it moving, don't be about telling me what they said, let's talk about why they were comfortable saying it in front of you in the first place.* Kill that Egyptian!

'Speak No Evil'

As I earlier said, we cannot always blame the lack of progress in our lives on other people. The things that we hide behind and our seemly stoic personalities, are the ones that determine whether we will achieve our God-given destiny or not.

Confront those areas of your life you have been protecting – the compensating behaviours you hide behind whenever you face the prospect of 'killing the Egyptian'. However mindful we have to be about people or other external factors, I have found that the most important growth we need to nurture is the one that takes place on the inside of us. Our internal monologues determine what comes out of our mouths, and eventually, our lives start to go in the 'direction' of our own words.

So, do not speak "evil". If you still are, that is an indication that you have not dealt with the hurts yet. Unresolved inner conflicts can have a detrimental effect on the words coming from our mouths. There was a time when I used to talk about the pain of the rejection from my dad's family, at every opportunity I could get. I was like a broken record, repeatedly reliving the hurt. I was living for the day when that side of the family would make amends for what they had done to me, but to my disappointment, this never happened.

I look back now, and I see the futility of my behaviour, at the time. Why was I wasting my time telling people who had hurt me, over and over, what they had done? To me, their actions were not trivial – it was not a case of a careless word, here and there, or being absent at a special occasion, none of that – but I can tell you that how they behaved towards me scarred me to the very core of my being. I wanted some form of restitution so badly, thinking that it was going to ease the pain I felt. I was wrong! There was no admission of guilt on their part. I have, on reflection come to accept things as they are. I realise now that 'killing the Egyptian' did not necessarily mean me soliciting an apology but deciding to stop re-enacting my past.

When you arrive at that point, at which you can unequivocally say, *"I will not let the past become my permanent address"*, that is the point at which you can rest assured that the Egyptian that held you captive, is dead.

For me, there were very clearly identifiable 'Egyptians' in my life that I needed to get rid of permanently! These (below) are some of the Egyptians that I have since had to get rid of:

- The Egyptian (people, systems, and the inner voices) that had imposed limitations on my life, telling me how high up they thought I could fly.

- The Egyptian in the form of anxiety that was stopping me from stepping out into new horizons, because I was afraid I would fail.

- The Egyptian that deemed me unfit to 'bat on their team'.

- The Egyptian that chose to overlook my intrinsic value because I didn't look or speak a certain way.

What is more, there are other Egyptians that I realise I still need to get rid of. Essentially, the day that I realised that this process was also about me dying to my past, was the day that the giants I have mentioned above, plus many others, began to fall in my life; one by one and slowly but surely.

Bury the thing

It is also very telling that Moses did not just kill his victim; he went ahead and buried him. I fail to comprehend why Moses chose to hang around the crime scene, considering what he had just done. Maybe he wanted to make sure the oppressor was truly dead and to put the *object of hurt* in his people's lives, and indeed his own, in a place where it would be difficult or impossible to find it.

Moses' further action in concealing the body of his victim symbolises the end of one era, and the beginning of another. Putting the dead Egyptian in the sand is a way of saying, *"I will not let the oppressor have the best of me ever again"*.

In our own lives, we need to 'bury' the persecutors by making sure we have eliminated the voices linked to the emotions or behaviours that they caused.

My husband and I have been going through what I will call an, *'airport season'* as we both are currently working and living on two separate continents.

Between us, we have been through a lot of airport departure lounges as well as immigration procedures and numerous flights. My travel preferences are very straightforward. I just get on the plane, sit, and get the food on offer; lights off, everyone silent, whilst I sleep. My next plan of action is to wake up a few hours before the plane touches down. Surely, this cannot be that hard, or is it?

Anyway, I was on one of my numerous journeys to visit my husband when I found myself on what I will call *a flight from hell.* It was in the middle of the Easter holidays, the flight was full of families – parents and kids, going to various holiday destinations.

The conversations in the cabin were in different languages, and at different pitches, throughout the seven and a half, or so hours flight – I was going mental! I had to find a way to quieten the noise.

I figured that to manage the *commotion* and everything else, that was going on in my head, I needed to tune in to a different frequency.

So, I opted to listen in, to a conversation between two friends sitting two seats ahead of me. Zoning into this conversation and blocking out all other sounds helped to quieten down the noise.

This experience led me to the theory that life must be like a big radio, but with different voices and opinions competing for attention. The frequency I chose to tune into, determined the voices I was listening to, and the music that dictated my dance. Choosing what frequency we turn on, is our responsibility, as it determines the type of sound to which we ultimately respond.

We must be alert to what we permit to speak into our lives. If not careful, you will find yourself tuned in to different frequencies – cynicism, criticism, self-doubt and discouragement, if you keep on holding on to the past. Therefore, you have a choice as to what station you choose to subscribe to. I have learned to tune my frequency to hope, trust, confidence, gentleness, and self-belief.

One of my favourite bible verses is Jeremiah 1:5 (MSG) and it says this:

> "Oh yes, you shaped me first inside, then out; you formed me in my mother's womb. I thank you, High God—you're breathtaking! Body and soul, I am marvellously made! I worship in adoration—what a creation! You know me inside and out, you know every bone in my body; You know exactly how I was made, bit by bit, how I was sculpted from nothing into something".

A Death

One of the reasons why some people fail to achieve their purpose and destiny is because they are too attached to who they have been. We must be willing to die to every form of false self to become that person that we were divinely designed to be.

I hear it all the time, and I may have said it myself time and again, "I've always been this way", really? Well, how is it working for you so far then?

As for me, when found out who I was called to be, different from the person I had seen every time I looked in the mirror, I said, *"enough"!* It was time I killed the Egyptian!

You must be willing to give up the false ideas of how your life should be, and who the person *progress-blockers* around you, think you should be, to discover the real you.

This process requires faith, and faith in a big God! Remember, God will always be gracious to us, as he takes us through such a journey. He leads us one-step at a time and stopping periodically to assess where we are. In due course, we discover who we really are.

Whatever thing we continuously give power to, will eventually manifest in our lives; so, do not let your negative past limit your personal development.

Remember, life is too short to keep holding on to the things that you should be getting rid of.

Chapter 6

USE YOUR WINGS

Sometimes it is easy to think that we have dealt with the issues that have held us captive in life. We may think we have *'killed the Egyptian'* and *'buried it'*, but painful memories can settle like a poison causing toxicity in our lives, left unchecked.

It is important, whether mentally or physically to separate from the hurt. To be able to achieve this, the decision or outcome must come from you. I have learnt that the greatest weapon we have in life is the ability to make choices. What I am saying is that challenging circumstances can only change by our ability to choose a different path in life. Not being able to make a choice is a complete waste of the power that is entrenched in those same choices. There is an old myth that says, "Frogs will pull down other frogs trying to escape the pot of boiling water". This may be stuff of *folklore*, but the dynamic is real in our lives. There will always be people who resist any form of change and who threaten to sabotage any attempt to self-improve.

What now?

So, you have 'killed' and 'buried the Egyptian,' but, *what now?*

You need to see progress in your life. If you are stuck in one place and the "*grass is not greener*", then you are potentially dying, and it is time to use your *wings*!

You will need to keep your feet on the ground but let your heart soar as high as it can. Resist the urge to be average or to surrender to the boundaries set by your environment.

Once I had identified and began to deal with the *'Egyptians'* in my life, I discovered that I had *wings* and that I was meant to fly, and to aim high; to soar to *unbelievable heights*, to reach for the *unreachable*, and achieve what *they* had said was *impossible*. A word that encouraged me in this season was a verse that I love in Proverbs 15:24, that says:

The path of life leads upward for the wise; they leave the grave behind.

This passage encourages me in the seasons where I feel discouraged about the difficulties I face in my quest to become who I was called to be. It helps me to look at my life and to anticipate my progression from past hurts, to reach for places I have never dreamt possible.

But I had to make sure that I was not afraid to go against the *'grain'*, and because I had *'killed'* the unhealthy desire to be *'accepted'*, the need for something greater, became stronger. Going against the flow, however, will cause controversy. I found this out, the hard way.

My decision to use my *wings,* to shatter the limitations and walk in my freedom was considered rebellious by some people.

This was saddening to me as this could not have been further from the truth. *Life* has taught me that whenever you are about to do something new, the people that limited you will reject it. However, you must make sure that the desire for approval does not hold more power than the need to do something fresh.

I personally discovered that *walking* in who I was made to be, helped me to walk *that little bit taller*! I was able to speak *that little bit firmer,* about the things that mattered to me. That was because my voice had found its confidence.

Like Moses, after killing the Egyptian, he found two fellow Israelites fighting. You would think that they had received enough beatings from their oppressors, not to turn on each other! Moses rebuked them, but they rejected his leadership.

We read in Exodus 2:13-15:

> The next day he went out there again. Two Hebrew men were fighting. He spoke to the man who started it: "Why are you hitting your neighbour?" The man shot back: *"Who do you think you are, telling us what to do? Are you going to kill me the way you killed that Egyptian?"* Then Moses panicked: "Word's gotten out—people know about this." Pharaoh heard about it and tried to kill Moses, but Moses got away to the land of Midian. He sat down by a well.

Afterwards, Pharaoh heard about what Moses had done and made a threat on his life. It was then that Moses *'took to the hills'* for fear of a reprisal from Pharaoh. He had no idea what was going to happen to him. Moses had left everything that he had known for the forty years of his life; he was using his wings!

Fleeing for his life must have made Moses think that God's plan for his life had completely been defeated. He possibly believed that every chance he had ever had, to deliver his people, was now over.

Little Moses know that at this point, he was right where God wanted him to be.

Using your wings, therefore, is less about running away from your past and more about running towards your destiny; it is about valuing yourself more than the need for peoples' acceptance. It is not about how badly *they* treated you, but more about understanding that what is in you, is good enough to be used, with, or without *their* approval.

In my life, it was liberating to look at myself and say, *"Enough is enough"!* I realised that every move I made was linked to my confidence and self-esteem. I wholeheartedly embraced the fact that I deserved better.

There are key lessons that I have identified in the process of using my wings. I discovered that *taking flight*:

- Would separate me from people, places and systems that were not working in my life.

- Would require a shift in the way that I was operating. I needed to accept my value and acknowledge, to myself at least, that I deserved better.

- Could only happen if I stopped hoping that *'they'* would *"see"* me.

- Would require that I let go of the search for *what they could be* to me, and accept who *they were,* presently, in my life.

I stopped adjusting who I was, to try and please people, and I stopped making excuses for why *they* were treating me the way they were; *I was flying now!*

You too, like me, could be struggling to *fit in* or to spread your *wings* in the environment you are in, currently. The keys I share may appear simple, and probably common sense to some, however, when you are caught in a cycle of *adjusting, excusing,* and searching for external validation, you can be blinded to even the simplest of solutions.

In my field of work, in the early days, I found it hard to break into the corporate world even though I was a qualified professional, trying to build a career for myself. I remember I spent my time licking stamps for envelopes I was using for the numerous job applications. It took me years to finally break into the job market. Eventually, after a very long and slow progression towards my goal, I found myself in a particular organisation, in a very senior position. In my mind, I had made it! This is what I had dreamt of. The frustration I had gone through was worth it; at least that is what I thought. I was in this job for a couple of years, loving life, when my line manager *'disappeared'!* And as quickly as she left, a new one was instated.

Looking back, the sudden *"disappearance"* of my manager and the rapid reinstatement of a new one should have been a red flag for me. If I could now pinpoint a moment that shifted the direction, I was moving in, in this organisation, this would have been it. This situation changed the dynamics of my work experience. It is difficult to explain just what it was like, but if I can say anything about her, it would be this; she must have graduated top of her class in the "school of micromanagers"!

I found *'new manager'* lacking in many departments, but I will spare you the details. The most annoying thing for me though was her tendency to operate with very little integrity! I really want to say zero integrity here, but I will refrain. I will say this though; if she was not a zero, then she was *cutting it really fine*!

Life in this organisation became difficult for me after this. The place had a culture of honouring the *'suck up'*, and I was not one of those. I have never been very good at *sucking up*; I guess this maybe the reason why I was in this predicament! I believe *'sucking up'* has nothing to do with honour. I have noticed, though, that this sort of behaviour is encouraged in some places, with a promise of *elevation* to some sort of prominent position. My belief is that any leader encouraging this is probably dealing with deep-seated insecurities that can only be validated by such a practice. As for the sucker up?

I think it is more about saying, *"I will do anything for you, even at the expense of others, so that in return, you reward me"!* True Honour will elevate, respect and serve, expecting nothing in return. I prefer honour!

My boss started her *campaign of terror* towards me, and it was hard to do anything that could satisfy her. The hours I invested into this organisation, even at the expense of my family, were not enough to make her happy! Over time, she collaborated with one of my subordinate managers, who because of this *partnership,* felt empowered to disrespect and disregard me, with impunity.

For the purpose of this story, I will call this subordinate, *'Dis'.* This name is short for *'disillusioned'.* 'Dis' decided he could do my job better than me. I disliked Dis, the most, in this *terror partnership,* if I was to be honest. This was because I had worked with him for years before *new manager* joined us. I had supported Dis through difficult times as his boss, and he knew better; I had been nothing but kind to him.

I am being factual about this season of my life and yet revisiting it in writing, reminds me of how hard this time was for me. When people turn against you, it can be soul devastating. The thing with life's journeys is that all of us will suffer at least one bad betrayal, in our lifetime. This is what unites us as people. The lessons we usually tell ourselves in retrospect are not to let the incidents destroy our trust in others, I truly believe this to be true. You must hold on to what you believe to be true about yourself; do not let others take that from you.

I remember working and writing emails well after midnight, trying to reduce my work pressure, in the hope of creating time to please my manager whilst I was present in the office. There were many times when I had not even logged out of my computer to sleep, when 'new manager' would respond in a very terse and dismissive manner, leaving me in an increased state of anxiety. Side note: I look back now, and I wonder why we were even talking to each other through emails, after office hours. If you are one of those doing this now, please stop it! The very fact that you are communicating with someone from work, deep in the dead of night, should be a massive red flag to your wellbeing.

Every time I turned on the computer and I heard the sound that is associated with it powering up, I would get that feeling you get in the stomach when you are petrified. This feeling would stay with me long after I had left the organisation. It took ages for me to get over the fear of the sound of the computer powering up! I see now how the computer, for me, became associated with feeling overwhelmed, and anxious, even long after I had left the organisation.

The straw that broke the camel's back

I was in one of the many meetings with *'new manager'* where she was presenting work that she had plagiarised from me. She went through this particular presentation and came to the section on the agenda that required those in attendance to ask questions, if they had any. She well and truly *tanked!* Why would she not, considering that she had not done the work that she was passing off as her own?

The more vicious the crowd became the more embarrassing it became for her. She turned to me, and said, *"Maybe Leah can come up and take these questions."* I do not know what came over me, but in hindsight, it was probably God shoving me out of that place. I piped up and responded, *"No you are good, you've got this"*!

I once read a quote that said, *"Wise people are not always silent, but they know when to be"*. I could have done well to remember this quote when in not so many words I told *"new manager" where to go*. What I was certain about, at that moment, however, was that it was time to go! How could I stay, after that?

God had given me so many opportunities to, *"kill this Egyptian, and to Use my wings"*, but I had been too intimidated with the whole situation, to do anything about it. That place had slowly been chipping away at my self-confidence and changing who I was.

It was then that I remembered to constantly remind myself of the fact that, no matter the challenges we face in life, we all have 'something' deep within us, that we can reach down into. That *something* is there to help us find an inner strength to win. I recognise now, that despite the difficulties I may face, I can choose to look at my life and say, *"this is not how my story ends"!*

It did not take long after this incident, when one day, whilst at my desk, at work, I stood up, picked up my handbag, took my family photos, my *special mug* off my desk, and I walked out. I did not know what the future held, but I was sure this was the end of this chapter for me. Had I not walked out, I would have eventually done something I would have truly regretted.

Overnight, I was unemployed, and I had lost my income. I felt pushed out; I felt *hard done by*. Despite this, I was comforted by the knowledge that I had used my *power* of *choice*. The decision I needed to make, was between trying to make sure my bills were paid and losing my self-respect and sanity. I chose the latter, and never looked back. You will find that everything in life, has a price, and sometimes that price is not always in form of money. Knowing when to walk out, *to use my wings,* was *powered* by wisdom. Being able to walk out, however? *That took courage!*

Faith made me walk out that day; faith in the form of my husband, who encouraged me, and reminded me to hold my head up high, push my shoulders back, and walk out with my dignity intact.

So, I can understand how Moses felt as he sat by the well after he had fled from Pharaoh! He must have been unsure of what would become of his life. Just like when I left my job, I had to learn to wait on God, to direct my next steps. The wait was quiet, but it was in *the wait,* that I had to dig *'wells of faith'.* Also, it was in the gap, between leaving my job, and finding my next assignment, that I turned to my faith, to discover once again, who I was, and what I was called to do!

Bounce

Exactly three weeks after I had left my job, I set up my own business. It was a modest *'one-man band',* but I was my own boss, I could pick my contracts, and I loved it! I had preserved my self-respect and in turn, found true freedom.

A few years after leaving, I was in a department store when I looked across, only to see an aged woman, in oversized shoes, scurry to hide, away from me, behind some racks of clothes! It was, *'new manager'!* I would like to say that seeing her like that brought me healing, but it did not. Healing could never come from her, but it would come from the internal decisions I would make; to allow myself to walk away from what was done to me. So yes, it did not heal me, but it sure did give me satisfaction. It took everything within me, not to walk across, stop behind her, and tap her on the shoulder and say, *"remember me"?*

Seven years after I had started my own business, I took up a consultancy role in a different organisation. On my first day, I was introduced to the managers on my team. To my absolute shock and horror, one of these managers was 'Dis'! *Remember Dis?* It had been seven years since I had seen or even heard of him! *...Good to see you too, I thought, in my head!* We had both come full circle! It was tempting to make him suffer, but I chose not to. He left soon after I got there; I guess his conscious got the better of him!

At times, we need to go outside of our *environment* to *see more clearly*. The day we take a good look at ourselves through the lens of self-belief and acceptance, is the day we begin to ascend slowly to the top.

For Moses too, time would come for him to face his past; he would face Pharaoh. He would face his past in a position of strength and demand that his people be released.

Chapter 7

GREEN GRASS, BLUE SKY

Everyone has a story to tell, and every life is a form of tapestry. When I started writing this book, my aim was to, just tell my story. In its genesis, however, it became clear that my experiences where not unique. I discovered that many people could relate to what I had for a long time, thought was an experience that was unique to me. It became clear that the lessons I had gathered along the way could become beneficial to someone on a similar journey. Because of that, I realised that what I was sharing, was more than just documented facts.

I am not an expert at life's issues, I am just a girl sharing her experiences, revelation and tools that led to my freedom. I find that the desire for freedom is universal, but many of us still hate to pursue it. Freedom comes with a price tag. It involves letting go of certain people, revaluating your attitudes and challenging certain behaviours. All this contributes to the price you will have to pay to obtain to your freedom. It will take time and you will have to go through a process.

We all want to be free, I guess, whether we are conscious of it, or not. I have found that society however, has moved to what I like to call, a *microwave operation*. We seem to want *what we want, yesterday*! There is a danger in this, because looking at my story, one would think that the change, and growth I talk about, happened rapidly.

In this chapter, I want to debunk that myth that says desired changes come as quickly as an Instagram quote. This approach is important, because it does not matter how much we discover *who we are,* visible change mostly comes slowly. I have come to appreciate that slow change is sustainable.

In this waiting season, I have had to lean on my faith in God. By nature, I do not like waiting. I do not like waiting in line, I do not like waiting for someone to call me back, I do not like it, but I am a work in progress. I learnt to wait on God for direction in life. The faith journey can be rough at times, and many times, I felt like I metaphorically had hopped on God's knee, and *'choked him out'*, looking for my answer.

I believe that God sometimes is deliberate when it appears to us, as if He is taking his time to answer our requests. This is because he may want to *perfect something* in us. There is something profound that we learn when time *slows down*, and we are put in a position where we have to wait for the miracle.

Just because you cannot see *fruit* yet, this does not mean that nothing is growing or happening on the inside of you.

Have you ever discovered something about yourself, which consequently made you to begin to put measures in place to effect change, but then you had to wait for that change to happen? Day after day, year after year, you wait, and still nothing happens? For me, after everything I have had to go through in my life, I now accept everything I lost. It has become clear to me, that it is important to make peace with what happened in my past. It also has been equally vital to ensure that I treasure what is left.

There are pivotal incidents in my life that have *'cut deep'*! After experiencing deep pain, I came to accept that I could not look at the things, and the people that had hurt me, and allow myself to be *stuck there*. This could only have come from a place of acceptance. I embraced what had gone on before, and only then did I begin to experience happiness. To achieve this, I had to delve into the deepest parts of my heart, to cultivate an atmosphere of tolerance and acceptance.

In some ways, I am still learning. By changing how I saw myself, I changed the narrative of my life. I was then able to say to my past hurts, *"you cannot control me anymore"!* This revelation also allowed me to accept that I was accountable for my life, and the choices I was making!

At first, I did not fully understand my transition, I had mistakenly thought that severing myself from toxic people and *'situations',* would automatically give me, *'blue sky, and green grass'!* It dawned on me that *life* does not work that way, as there was seemingly the requirement to wait for *things* to finally begin to change, for the better.

Starting something new is sometimes exciting. It gives us a *buzz* and an anticipation of what could be. Initially, progress may even appear rapid; it feels good, and because of that, it is easy to start believing in *our own hype*! But, sooner or later we get to the middle of this transition, and this phase is excruciatingly painful, because it appears as if nothing is happening, and no matter how much we try to change things, it feels as if we are stuck.

For me, because of what I saw as delay, I many times wanted to give up on what I knew I was purposed to do. Giving up is a choice, but I was also aware that this was an easy option. Waiting can at times cause you to develop self-doubt. It is sometimes easier to fight a battle when the enemy is visible, and on the outside. So, I seemed to be winning in terms of, 'sifting the opinions front'. But self-doubt was a different battle all together. I was not sure I knew how to fight this one.

The most valuable piece of advice I have ever been given, is to persevere, to keep pushing. Besides, it is a known fact that something 'good' always comes from situations that really place a *demand* on you!

So now, rather than battling the narrative that had been programmed into me by others, I started playing a self-composed *symphony* that was telling me I did not qualify. All this was driven by the fear to step out and start again, with a new vision of what I was called to do.

In these circumstances too, I grew; learning that the perspective of the issues I was facing, was probably more problematic, than the difficulties surrounding my transition to becoming my authentic self. I have had many worries in my life. Over time, I have come to realise that a majority have never even materialised.

Shadows will always chase you; it is part of the journey, but you must be careful not to let them overwhelm and overcome you.

Moses must have felt similar emotions as he sat *waiting,* in Midian. In Exodus2:15 it says,

> "When Pharaoh heard of this, he tried to kill Moses, but Moses fled from Pharaoh and went to live in Midian, where he sat down by a well. Now a priest of Midian had seven daughters, and they came to draw water and fill the troughs to water their father's flock. Some shepherds came along and drove them away, but Moses got up and came to their rescue and watered their flock".

The land of Midian was where Moses spent forty years in exile, after he had committed murder. He left behind everything he knew and found himself *sitting* by a well. He was probably struggling to come to terms with life as it now was. And I am sure that at some point, Moses must have questioned himself as to what had happened. How did a prince end up sitting by a well, in the scorching sun, and with nothing to show for it?

Moses had previously known nothing but the privileged life of the palace. It must have been tempting to look back and long for the times he had lived as royalty. Did he remember how his *"brothers"* had rejected his leadership? Did he perhaps ask himself whether it was all worth it?

When we too hit the proverbial *"road block"*, we can be in danger of thinking that we are stuck, forever. We then spend our lives feeling immobilised; thinking about how we will escape one day and how *awesome* that will be.

But, we should draw on the one thing that no one can steal from us, our dreams! Imagine yourself as a fighter, and you are in the ninth round, of a ten-round fight. Unfortunately, your opponent has you backed into the ropes, you turn for a second, and bang, he *clocks you one!* You are down on the canvas, and the referee is now *counting you out.* In these situations, you must remember, *'you might be down, but you are not out for the count'!* You can turn matters around. Your legs may wobble, but you must tell yourself you are going to get up, and you are going to finish the fight. Not only are you going to finish the fight, you must purpose in your mind, that you are going to win.

Society's most current and popular message encourages us to walk away, when things appear not to be working. It is easy to be sucked in to this position. However, in my case, it dawned on me that maybe there was an alternative to this message. Rather than walking away when things became difficult, I mustered the power to stay, to look at my transition, and keep going because it was worth *sticking at* it. Fighting to the very end demonstrates resilience; it outlines the ability to embrace the beautifully broad spectrum of your experiences, and to ensure you have learnt from them.

Your *world* will *bend* sometimes, it will not look like you want it to, but you must keep in mind that it is all part of the process. And, the power lies in knowing the difference between something that is '*just bent*', and what is completely *broken!*

Wait a minute!

I have been in situations where I have held on to my dreams for a long time, yearning for them to come to fruition; the *waiting game,* however, takes its toll. In a situation like this, time can look like it is ticking by, slowly, and sometimes it may appear as if nothing is really changing!

Desperation then creeps in, and you may even panic a little bit, because it feels as if time is running out. It is moments like these where it is easy to think that maybe the time has come to let go of a dream, and the hope or aspiration of something new. But this is not true; *just because you cannot see it yet, it does not mean nothing is happening!* In this process, I discovered that God might answer our requests in three ways:

- "*No.*"
- "*Wait a minute.*"
- "*Yes, go!*"

It was during this period of my life, that I looked around at the people in *my world,* and mistakenly thought that because they were influential individuals, they could give me a helping hand that would propel me into my future. The only thing is, when it came to giving themselves to assist me, to fulfil my dream? *they never came through for me!*

I was hurt, I harboured offence, and I struggled with not apportioning blame on *them,* for *perceived* failure. I was walking around as if I had it all together, and yet inside, I was completely *crumbling!*

When things like these happen, you have two choices. You can become *bitter,* or you can become *better.* Choose the latter; it takes just one a step at a time! I learnt that the only revenge that I was meant to focus on was to achieve my dreams!

There is nothing more painful than recognising that you *carry something* in you that can add value in your circles, and yet the people in your world refuse to acknowledge it. Trying to prove something to people who deliberately refuse to pay you some attention depletes your self-worth, and respect.

It is senseless to devolve responsibility for my ultimate purpose in life into someone else's hands.

Life has its ups and downs, *it is just the way it is.* Imagine if we all got what we wanted, all the time;

no struggle, no hard work, and no challenges. As amazing as this may sound, it would mean no growth! It is just like a work out in the gym. Where there is no resistance, there can be no strength.

I am not advocating for more struggles, I am merely pointing out the positives of experiencing *'the waiting'*, that goes together with the dreams we hold in life. I cannot tell you the countless times I have cowered, biting my nails and wanting to give up on many fronts. But, like I have said repeatedly, I refused to back down; *I just kept turning up!*

Sometimes, our struggle to reach our goals and dreams is not because we are failing, it is because we stop at the first *hurdle* we encounter. Those who succeed refuse to stop because something is *failing*; they find ways to *rescue it*! This can be a relationship, a business, a career or lifelong dreams. When we do not succeed, it is not because we failed. We fail because we stop trying! Failure is not the end of the story; it is the start of *a comeback*.

Thinking about the gap between my dreams and their fruition made me remember an illustration of a *'Pilot, a Plane, and a Ground controller'*, When a pilot takes off from any airport; he or she has a destination in mind. In flight, the plane goes through various *protocols* and *actions* that will take it to where the pilot wants to go. Eventually, the pilot has the destination in sight, indicated by the '*chequered flag*', confirming arrival at a destination.

As the pilot approaches the intended destination, he or she begins the landing '*preparations*'. At this stage, there is constant communication with the Ground controller, issuing guidance on how, where, and when they should land.

The pilot cannot see the ground and so totally relies on the controller to guide him or her. In the event that the ground conditions are not conducive for landing, the controller says these words, to the pilot, "*maintain holding pattern until you are instructed to go*". The pilot then flies in a set pattern, hovering over the destination, whilst waiting for direction from the ground as to when it is right to land.

Like a plane's holding pattern, our transition period is God's way of saying, "wait *a minute*"! At times, like a pilot, it may appear as if we are circling the same spot, waiting with nothing to show for it. However, the ground controller has more visibility and understands the landing conditions better than the pilot does. Our lives are more like the pilots, and the controller is like God, telling us when it is the right time to land.

In Psalms 5: 3, David says:

"Listen to my voice in the morning, LORD. Each morning I bring my requests to you and wait expectantly".

So, for everyone who has a dream, wait expectantly. Our dreams can change us and change the world around us. We may also need to reconsider our outlook on our future, to live out the highest version of who we were called to be. Dreaming is simply exploring the possibilities; for the *impossible* to become the *possible.*

I find that children for example do not put limitations on what they can do or achieve. They tend to dream bigger than their circumstances, at any given moment. When my daughter was younger, she always used to tell me how she wanted to be a 'sky scrapper'! It did not matter how many limitations I put on her, she was going to be one!

Of course, she did turn out to be a *sky scrapper* – thank God! The point I am trying to illustrate is that we must operate in the realm of numerous possibilities, and not let our mental limitations contain us. Remember, *blue skies, green grass!*

We know from history that some of the biggest dreamers have brought about the most lasting, and positive changes. The ability to dream makes anything possible. Imagining a desirable future is what keeps us going!

Actually, the word, *"Imagination"*, originates from the word, *"Image"*. *It is a synthesis of images that form new ideas, that eventually turn into dreams, if we explore them!* Having a positive image of oneself, is, therefore, an open door to greater imaginations.

As you go through life working towards your dreams, knowing who you are, and who you aspire to be, will be the key to your success. Having said that, becoming who you ought to be, is never easy. It requires tremendous courage, perseverance, and a steadfast belief in yourself.

You *must* believe success is possible. Because as you continue your journey, you *will* eventually embark upon those moments, the ones that you have always imagined would come true. What we aim to become must always be authentic, only then can we grow fully into who we were meant to be. It is folly to try to imitate something just because we have seen it work for someone else! The position we should take is that of constantly challenging ourselves with the *"whys"* of our desires.

Author Richard Bach once wrote:

> *"You are never given a dream without also being given the power to make it true".*

So, no matter how discouraged you might get at times, you must remember that if you can dream something, then you already have everything in you, to make it come true.

Chapter 8

FLYING IN FORMATION

It came to a point in my life where I was clear about the people, situations and triggers that were detrimental to me. I had for a long time tried to rationalise, excuse and to an extent, tolerate behaviours and opinions.

But, I had reached my limit. I came to accept, fully, that yearning for external validation and acceptance was a futile exercise, once *their* minds had been made up. I repeated this statement to myself over, and over again, until I began to believe it. I was training myself not to live for other people's approval and validation.

I now had a new mantra in life that said, *"I do not care what they think"!* It is okay, I guess, to remind yourself not to rely too much on external factors to get you where you need to be. The downside to this, however, is that this mantra can make you feel isolated, and in some cases, a little paranoid that *"someone is out to get you"!*

It is so easy to see an enemy, *everywhere*, if that is all you are looking for. The thing is this; we cannot always put the blame on other people for the perceived lack of progression in our lives, however dysfunctional they may behave! One of the things I have learnt in life is that, before we can conquer any external challenges, we will first have to master inner battles. If we do not, self-doubt will creep into our system when we least expect it, and before we know it, there is a full-blown war going on in our heads and we are not even aware of it.

I had *calibrated* my life, and I was ready to emerge *kicking and fighting*! My mission, as I saw it, was to fulfil my purpose and not to pander to my critics. I had wasted a lot of my time waiting around for permission. However, I was dreaming again, I was flying beyond any previous limitations. I wish, however, that this was the answer to the *"meaning of life"*, but unfortunately, for me, it was just the beginning. I saw myself as a *warrior*, fighting for my position in life. I fought, to prove to myself and to others that I was worth something. I was confrontational with people, and with systems that

I saw as prejudicial towards persons like me. There were countless times I remember, when the words and actions of others would injure me.

I tried to *educate* them, hoping that they would understand why their actions where hurtful. Then I had a *"eureka"'* moment! People will keep hold of the narrative they are most comfortable with, and you cannot teach people who are not willing to learn.

I was going through life trying to make *right,* all the *wrongs* that I saw in my world. When you try to *recalibrate* the *scales* of what you think are the imbalances in the way people treat you, you can only fix them as far as your own human understanding can take you. I had to settle for the fact that some people do not require educating, they rather require a *heart transformation*, and only God can do that! I also read somewhere, and it said; *"there is no greater inequality than the equal treatment of unequals".*

Taking matters into our own hands is counterproductive. It ties you to offences that should be in your past. In your quest for parity, you end up stuck in a loop of pain, and it never stops. We, therefore, need take care that we do not become the very thing that we have been criticising! To salvage my inner peace and state of mind, I let go of the *stuff* that had held me back. This act helped me to restore my balance, in all areas of my life. It allowed me to take my hands-off situations and this freed me from unnecessary stress thus trusting God to deal with them.

The Great Equalizer

Doing things in my own strength was an exhausting process. It was only when it dawned on me that I had a gift that I had been underutilising, that I activated my faith, in this area of my life. Irrespective of the *"imbalanced scales"*, you have faced in life, God can, and will right them. He is the great equalizer!

In Proverbs 16:11 the bible states that:

> "The LORD demands accurate scales and balances; he sets the standards for fairness".

Reading this was a huge relief for me! Even though this scripture in its context refers to matters of commerce, it clearly communicates who it is that sets the standards of fairness - God. It was an incredible feeling when I finally realised that it was not my job, but Gods. He is hugely invested in justice and it is an affront to him, to go against this principle, by doing *wrong,* under the pretence of doing *right.* The scales are his invention. God has put into the heart of men the ability to keep and to maintain truth and justice, in the affairs of life.

This capability is within us. It is up to us to choose right from wrong. When God begins to redress the inequities, He creates a level playing field, removing any man-made advantages. Even Moses experienced this, he saw God delivering his people from bondage, after a seemingly long period of unfairness.

Eventually, and one way or another, the rebalancing will happen. God does not have to do it, because He must, he does it because He is who He is!

When you hand over your challenges to God, you discover just what a great equalizer He is.

Romans 3:21-24 (MSG) puts this point so concisely:

> "But in our time something new has been added. What Moses and the prophets witnessed to all those years has happened. The God-setting-things-right that we read about has become Jesus-setting-things-right for us. And not only for us, but for everyone who believes in him. For there is no difference between us and them in this".

I love the fact that this passage says, *"In our time, something new has been added"!* The day that I understood this verse, it encouraged me immensely. It gave me confidence that there was something new happening in my time, something different to the challenges I had faced. It was the *setting* of *things* right. This understanding allowed me to concentrate on *'becoming'* rather than *'correcting'*.

Abdicating my purpose because I was busy doing something else would by default permit other people to decide who I was. You see, as we go through life, there is a danger that we can just become more and more like everyone else. I wanted to decide that for myself. I wanted to avoid becoming too *'styled'*, too *'done'*, and too generic.

Knowing Me, Knowing You

As I mentioned in earlier chapters, I was a girl who had a *'mouth'* on her! It was something I battled with, most of my life. Not because I did not like my *'talking'*, it was because it was inferred as problematic for a large part of my growing up! In the end, however, I was able to embrace it; I came to accept it when I understood that God deliberately and intricately moulded me in this way, for His use. As He Himself says in Jeremiah 5:1:

> "I knew you before I formed you in your mother's womb. Before you were born I set you apart and appointed you as my prophet to the nations".

I love how this scripture clearly puts it; the fact that I was just the way God wanted me to be – no regrets, no mistakes. The pep talk I gave myself was this; "I am *known*; I was created with my quirks and idiosyncrasies, precisely to fulfil my future".

Not only was I was called to *'talk'*, but there also came a *'Divine revelation'*, that the same applied in my *professional life*, as it did in my *personal life*. I spoke a lot in my professional career, conducting large workshops and conferences, and as a *speaker*, this should have been enough for me. So why was I still feeling unsatisfied? Why did I feel unfulfilled? If "speaking" and communicating with people was the sum total of my purpose, then this should have made me complete, but it did not!

It was this internal conflict that led me to realise that whatever gifts we have can only be fulfilled when they are used for a purpose greater than ourselves. I wanted to speak and to change lives. I wanted to use my voice to speak into situations, cultures, and see things change. I wanted to help lives!

The problem with having a *'microphone gift'* though, is that you may be in danger of being misunderstood as one who desires fame and loves the sound of one's *'own voice'*! In the beginning, I thought that to help people, with *my voice*, meant I was called to be a preacher, in a church. I have the greatest of respect for preachers. It is from preachers that I get the most growth.

For me, however, I discovered that *my voice* was not only for the church but also for the whole *world*. I knew I had to commit to pursuing my dreams, no regrets and distractions. However, following your dreams is not always all it is *cracked* up to be.

I think that watching movies has misled us, to some extent. We watch someone following their dreams on the screens, and the conventional narrative formula leads us to believe that after one or two hiccups, and a couple of hours, we will eventually get exactly what we want.

The real world operates somewhat differently. For some people, this dream path may pan out just the way they had envisaged it would. But for others, the road may be long and challenging. Pursuing dreams is often more rewarding, and more enlightening, than the achievement of the dreams themselves, at least that is what I learnt.

It took a long time for me to find my voice. Initially, I thought that there were steps one had to go through, like being invited to *platforms*. This is true to an extent, but in doing so, you became totally reliant on "man", to fulfil only what God can.

Left unchecked, you can find yourself trying to fit into existing systems, and structures without any real understanding of whether you belong there, or not. You end up jumping through hoops and get frustrated when things do not materialise. Before you know it, you feel like the world owes it to you, to make your life's dream happen! This is what you must watch out for, regardless of what it was that happened or did not happen to you. You need to guard your heart, ensuring that it does not become entitled to places, or people that God only wants to use to train you.

Romans 12:2 (NLT) gave me an epiphany. It says:

> "Don't copy the behaviour and customs of this world, but let God transform you into a new person by changing the way you think. Then you will learn to know God's will for you, which is good and pleasing and perfect".

Ping! That was my *'light bulb moment'!* The key was changing the way I was thinking about my future. I needed to *renew* my mind! No one owed me anything! God's will for me was *pleasing* and *perfect*.

Embracing this truth places you right in the middle of God's timing for you. It frees you from the expectations of others and gives you confidence in the fact that your future is secure, no matter how many setbacks you encounter!

At the time, I wrote this in my journal:

> *"Lord I have come to the end of myself! I have spent an enormous amount of time, 'working' for acceptance, chasing a standard that was never designed for me. I see now through different lens. I see that just because I am not designed for it, it does not mean I was not qualified to be here. It just means I was never part of the story. I have lost*

a lot of energy trying to figure out the "whys" of this truth. Does it mean I am not loved? Does it mean I am not good enough? But actually none of this is true. I am a queen.

Leah remind yourself that your faith is in control. Your best strategy cannot, and will not come from a place of fear, inadequacy, or insecurity. No one owes you anything; recognise that you need to carve out your own individual path! Make peace with this fact, embrace it. It is time to press forward, push some buttons, crash some doors and collide with destiny! The journey will be liberating and also isolating, don't give up. It takes a special kind of person to resist comfort, and to press into the unknown".

However painful it may have been, I learnt that I did not have to make-out someone to be a 'villain'. just because I had decided to let go of the 'idea' of who they could be to me. My job was to love everyone and to just let the 'great equaliser' do His job. My greatest comfort was knowing that the God I serve, was greater than the problems I had faced.

Formation

It has been said that those who achieve high levels of success require one key factor – consistency. To be consistent means to dedicate oneself completely to a task, activity or goal. This means that you must be without distraction, and fully engaged with where you want to go! You need to *"fly in formation"!*

For consistency to occur, however, it requires a commitment on our part. It necessitates that we commit ourselves to a sustained effort of action for the long haul. In other words, consistency is all about your ability to be dependable, reliable, and responsible for all your choices, decisions and actions regarding the outworking of your purpose.

Our everyday habits have a direct impact on our goals in life. I learnt, over time, that essentially, success comes down to your ability to hold yourself accountable for the daily choices you make. All responsibility lies solely in your hands. Personally, I was willing to allow myself to be a novice, at the next level of my progress towards my dreams, when I recognised that I had become experienced in the current one. *I was evolving, I was learning*! You can learn even from the most *'unlikely'* source, the most *'unlikely'* person or even the most *'unlikely'* situation if you are humble enough. You just need to keep showing up! Our habits can define us! They are powerful and are difficult to make or break. But, if you can gain control over them, you can forge yourself into the person you want to become. This, of course, is easier said than done!

Some people go through their whole lives without ever realising the fact that they can develop positive habits, or that they can succeed in breaking the ones that drag them down. There is no shortcut to mastering your behaviours. It takes discipline, time and hard work. Nevertheless, there is one principle that can guide you to a greater success rate. It is the idea that whatever we put our hands to, must be rooted in consistency.

The voice of change will taunt you with your fears and anxieties if you let it. *"What if I open myself up to disappointment again? What if I cannot do it well? What if it's harder than I expected, and I fail?"*

All these questions may plague you, but your job is to keep the *'format'*. *You need to fly in formation*, repeatedly, until you get a breakthrough!

Chapter 9

ENDING STRONG?

I used to wonder about the exact moment it dawned on Moses that his season in Pharaoh's palace was over. Was it when he killed the Egyptian or was it after he fled? Thinking about his life, I found it difficult to pinpoint exactly when Moses finally realised, that the end had come for him. It was then that I had an epiphany; that maybe, even in our lives, the end of a season is not an event, but it is rather a process.

I believe that the end of an era is not like a light switch that you flick off when you are about to exit a room. I somewhat think that the *end* comes gradually; it happens in steps. The word 'steps', for me, implies a gradual progress. It means that wherever it is we are going, it may take a while, but closing one door, to open the next, is inevitable!

What people see as the end of something, is probably not so. It is easy to write of an experience as complete, with very little understanding of the real story. I have also learnt that to define an end to a season, requires an understanding of the dynamics of any given situation. The end may not necessarily be tied to the things that we see, it may rather be hidden in the realm of the unseen.

The end of a season in our lives can be just as challenging as the start of a new one. Letting go of habits, thinking patterns, behaviours and people, can be difficult when that is all you have ever known. Similarly, in reading this book, you may look at some of what I perceive as my triumphs in life and think that I was strong in those times; but my victories did not come easily.

When we hear statements like, "let go of your past", we tend to think that this statement works like a magic wand and it will instantly resolve all our problems. But, I have learnt that is usually not the case. My observation has been that every breakthrough takes effort and discipline.

Ending a season strong has been more difficult than imagined, especially when the memories of the previous season have been challenging. Dark memories can be lurking in the shadows, holding you hostage to the worst possible version of yourself.

To walk into a season of victory, we must rearrange or even change certain things. We must identify what we need to change before we even start to think of the process that will get us from one position to the next.

We are always told that the key to a successful future is to end every season strong. Equally, it is assumed that the point, at which we stop, becomes the launch pad into the next new thing.

It makes sense I suppose until you look around, and notice that there are many seasons that physically seem not to have ended strong, and yet the very finishing was the strength in itself!

To help assess our progress fairly, it may also be helpful to understand that, what is perceived as finishing strong should also be viewed from a set of metrics that are not limited to the visual!

It is often said that you must conceive a thought in your mind first before you can ever act on it. For Moses, winding down of his time with Pharaoh must have started in the mind. He may have thought about it way before he acted.

In Hebrews 11:24-25 it says:

> "It was by faith that Moses, when he grew up, refused to be called the son of Pharaoh's daughter. He chose to share the oppression of God's people instead of enjoying the fleeting pleasures of sin".

Growing up is never instantaneous! It occurs when you discover your inner strength to weather the storms of life. It is only then that you find your turning point. For Moses, the above scripture tells us that it was "by faith" when Moses "grew up", that he decided the palace was not the place for him.
The killing of the Egyptian was probably the first, and physical manifestation of the process that led to the end of an era. Fleeing the palace, however, was drawing a line in the sand, to his former life. This was the point of no return!

Exodus 2:14-17 outlines how Moses finds himself in a place called Midian:

> Then Moses was afraid, thinking, "Everyone knows what I did." And sure enough, Pharaoh heard what had happened, and he tried to kill Moses. But Moses fled from Pharaoh and went to live in the land of Midian.
>
> When Moses arrived in Midian, he sat down beside a well.

So, Moses is now in Midian. It is inconceivable, to think that Moses' running away from Pharaoh could be considered as finishing strong, especially when we find him, a former prince, sitting by a well in Exodus 3.

'*A former prince, sitting by the well,*' with seemingly nothing to do, is hardly a position of strength! To top it all off, the word "fled", in this scripture also, does not give a picture of a confident Moses as he leaves!

There are numerous examples of situations that to us may appear to have ended in ways we would regard as failure and yet they are not. We have examples such as Moses fleeing from one place to the next and even Jesus on the cross, at Golgotha. Jesus looked nothing but strong when His time on earth, was finished! Things may have appeared not have ended well for him, and yet the death, at the cross, itself was an embodiment of strength. Moses went on to free the Israelites, and Jesus freed the whole of humanity.

The gift I gave to myself was to make sure that I used the correct measure to determine perceived success or failure, in every season I found myself. I needed to understand that all my experiences were unique to me, and therefore the ending would be equally bespoke to who I was. So, *cut yourself some slack*; *things* do not need to look like you are *winning* in order for you to see the ending as *strong*!

But tell me the reason

I had a friend I knew from my teenage years, we grew up together, changed, and morphed into older versions of ourselves. I call this person a *'friend'*, because that is what I thought they were to me, at that time. However, looking back, I am not sure that the word, *'friendship'*, would describe us. I see now how our relationship was rooted in dysfunction. I refer to them as, *'they,'* in this part of the book, because not only do I want to protect their identity, but also I am acutely aware that, they too may have their own perspective on how they saw our friendship.

My other friends used to encourage me to persevere in the friendship as it was purposed. I was not, and probably still not, sure what that purpose looked like for me! For me, the most challenging aspect of our relationship was that I was constantly walking on eggshells, double, and triple checking what I had said for fear of offending *them*. It did not matter how careful I was, offending *them* was inevitable, because, they, as far as I was concerned, had a *very 'thin skin'*.

The fear of 'offending' was not the only dysfunction; there was also, the absence of boundaries. I had long abandoned the idea of implementing any healthy boundaries in our relationship, as I was afraid that doing so was a sure way of *getting a telling off*!

An example of a boundary I desperately needed but was afraid to implement was when *they* would call me on the phone. If I were busy, I would state from the onset that I was a little busy, but it was as if my statement had fallen on deaf ears. Ever had one of those friends who call you, and you say you are busy, but two hours later they are still on the phone and you are yelling on the inside, *"I was busy two hours ago"*? *Was I crazy*? Two whole hours of my family time spent on the phone, with an individual who had no respect for my time or personal space?

I was a grown woman and yet when a call came through from *them* I was afraid to ignore it, but also equally nervous about answering it. You could usually tell from the first few seconds they were on the phone, whether they were unhappy with you, or not. I would then have this nervous knot in the base of my stomach because I really was not sure what I had done wrong. It was always something I or other people had done. However, I cannot, *'hand on heart'*, ever recollect a conversation where they had done a bit of introspection, and were willing to accept that they also may have injured me in some way.

One incident sticks out to me, to this day. On one occasion, they called me, out of the blue, to ask why my husband drove a *girl's car*! *A girl's car*? What did that even mean? What was it to her anyway? I still get angry thinking about it even now, because I wonder how I let my self-worth get so low as to have allowed someone to think they had the permission to insult my loved ones.

I remember how happy I was with that car until *they* made this comment. I thought, *"Now I am annoyed about something I was happy with before you opened your mouth"!* Sometimes, we unknowingly let discontentment creep into our hearts when we permit other people's words to permeate our souls.

Is it not funny how we can allow people into our lives and they end up, *adjusting the temperature and flip our furniture around* before they leave? I am training myself not to misplace my energy by getting annoyed at the negative opinions made about me, but rather ensuring that I am clear about the voices, I give permission to speak into my life.

I was a mother, with two little girls who were growing up quickly and were looking to me for guidance on how to form healthy friendships. But, here I was, afraid of speaking *my words.* I realised that if I did not get my act together, I would become a poor example of understanding our value and how to live authentically, to my kids.

The question I am usually asked when I tell this story is, *"why did you stay friends for so long"?* and the answer I honestly give is, *"I don't know"!* The lesson in this for me was that you could not *medicate* the thing that you cannot *diagnose.* In this friendship, I did not fully understand the root of my dysfunction, maybe I did not want to understand, I am not sure. Because I did not understand the *root* of the wrongs in our friendship, I could not change how I behaved. In hindsight, maybe I was aware, at times, of the toxicity of our relationship but I was petrified to confront it, and so I stayed silent. I suspect that acknowledging the *toxin* in this relationship, would have compelled me to do something, but I was not ready, I was afraid.

The diagnosis and consequent medication of any dysfunction are essential to the ability to heal from it. I discovered, however, that sometimes, the medication is tougher than the illness. I guess that is why I stayed '*unwell*', in this friendship, for so long.

You did what?

In this day of social media, I have learnt that people take their list of '*followers*' and '*friends*' super serious! I have even heard of people who purchase an application that enables them to track who *unfollows* or *unfriends* them on social media. I personally cannot get my head around the level of commitment it takes to track people on these sites. Anyway, one day, I did the unthinkable, for this particular friend, I pressed the unfriend button on my Facebook account!

To be honest, I did not put much thought into the action I took that day. I think I was just tired of the negativity and of how our conversations were *draining* me. Our encounters were getting more and more difficult for me. I look back now, and I see that I was not looking to end our friendship; I just wanted to reduce the channels through which I could hear from them.

Their response was to *'exterminate'* me from interacting with them, ever! They went all *thermonuclear* on me! Talk about using a sledgehammer to crack a nut. Even though I was taken aback by their reaction, I have the utmost respect for the fact that, they took a swift decision about our friendship the minute they had assessed they were not happy with it.

For me, our friendship ended abruptly. Even though the decision to end it was not mine, I am on reflection thankful, in that it helped me to end a nightmare episode in my life! Sometimes it takes a decision that originates outside of ourselves, to help us move on from a situation we are incapable of doing so. It saddens me to now realise that I did not have it within me to stand up for myself in this relationship. I am sure I am not alone; countless other people find themselves caught up in this same conundrum, *"how do I walk away without hurting anyone"*?

The answer to this question is this; you cannot walk away from any relationship without leaving some *collateral damage*. However, peace comes when you recognise who you really are in any relationship. Accept who *they* are in the relationship and not who you hoped *they* would be. Eventually, however, you will need to muster the power to implement healthy boundaries. Natural separations do occur in life, but our job is to simply pay attention, and not to try to tamper with the process.

The question in this instance is, *"did I end strong, or not"?* I am not sure what the correct answer is. But, I see now how when *they* ended our friendship, I was still able to close that part of my season, in strength. Their action made me evaluate myself again as a mother, wife, and as a person. I asked myself this question: *"what example was I setting to those close to me"?* Also, *"what was I tolerating and what impact did it have on those who were looking up to me"?*

Even though the separation in this case made sense, learning to live without *them,* was not easy. What is it that drew me to this state of negativity? Why was it seemingly easy for them to walk away, whilst I struggled? The actions I took, or I did not take, greatly reflected what was happening inside me.

Longing for *them* after they had left, was the greatest revelation of this story. What makes us want to stay, even when we know that something is *killing* us?

I think that the reasons why we do this are plenty. On a 'practical' level, one big aspect of this is attachment. We can get attached to other people, and to our environment. We also develop habits and get used to a given situation, resulting in a dislike for change. In the end, even if the situation we live in is not good for us, we are afraid to change it.

I tell this story to remind us not to lose heart, when it seems that a door has closed, and we find ourselves staring at the shut door, in what looks like failure. Remember, life is full of 'sentences', therefore, it is important that in your life's 'sentences' you do not put a 'full stop' where you are meant to put a comma. One of my favourite bible passages has this beautiful word of encouragement:

"And we know that God causes everything to work together for the good of those who love God and are called according to his purpose for them" Romans 8:28.

So, while it may look as though you have failed, it all works out in the end, trust me!

Chapter 10

IT'S NOT OVER, TILL IT'S OVER

My parents separated when I was in my teens. I am not sure why, but I think it had something to do with the pressure from the extended family. Besides, I was too preoccupied with *teenage hormones* to understand fully what had happened. I came back from boarding school one half-term and found that my mother and my siblings had moved in with her sister.

For some reason, my parents never divorced, and up until my father died, my parents remained 'friends'. In fact, my father usually stopped over for *'weekends'* at my mother's home, unbeknownst to his family, just to see us. Now that I am older, I look back at this scenario with amusement!

Does it have to be this way?

Families are interesting units. I somewhat believe that children are moulded by the culture of the family into which they are born. In my country of birth for example, certain cultures are either matrilineal or patrilineal. This simply means, among many other things, that a couple's children are entirely the responsibility of either the mother or the father. People outside of this culture may find this incredulous and I accept that. This is because there are many foreign cultural practices that I also find hard to grasp at times.

My father's culture is matrilineal. This means that I was supposed to be my mum's entire responsibility. My mother's family, however, were patrilineal, which was the total opposite of my father's. I was stuck in the middle; caught up in a *vortex*! Although this practice has evolved in the newest of generations, my father's relatives, however, chose to exercise their right to this culture, when dealing with my siblings and me.

From their perspective, my siblings and I had no business expecting any parental support, emotional, or otherwise, from my father. In their opinion, my dad was responsible for my paternal aunt's children. *Sounds crazy, right*? I spent many years fighting this archaic way of thinking!

I remember once, a group of my paternal family coming to my mother's house when my parents separated. They demanded that my mother should stop my siblings and I from spending time with my father. Their view was that we were a drain on my father's resources. You have to laugh, or maybe admire, a little, the audacity one has, to pull off such a request.

He did what?

As I mentioned earlier, my father's mental illness was one of the challenges my parents faced in their marriage. My mother had done a good job supporting, well, I call it *'concealing'*, my father's mental illness. She had tried to contain it within *intimate* circles. Looking at my experiences, and how I approached them, I see now how my mother's behaviour may have influenced my outlook on this aspect of my life. It taught me to hide my true feelings; I learnt to wear a *'mask'*, to hide my internal turmoil.

After my mother left my dad, it was impossible for her to conceal his illness. I was on edge all the time, mentally prepared for the bad, the ugly, and the very ugly, to go public, regarding my father's illness. My dad for the first time was not around us every day. Because of this, we could not control what *message* was going out to the world any more, but even I was not prepared for the ignorance that was spoken.

To me, my dad was just like any other father, on the face of it. It was just that at times, he would have these breakdowns. The problem with mental illness is that it lacks a *marker*, some sort of *barometer* that flashes to the world saying, *"go easy on me, I am not feeling too great"*.

I remember one episode; dad got dressed in a suit and headed out to *State House.* 'State House' is the name given to the stately homes that most African presidents' live in. My dad walked up to the guards who were patrolling the forbidding gates of this stately house and demanded to *speak* to the president. According to him, he had a few issues of national interest that he wanted to *iron out* with the head of state. In Africa, you cannot walk up to the state house with a list of hostile demands, and still, expect to hold to on your freedom! My father was arrested, at gunpoint!

We had a difficult time trying to convince the authorities that he was not well. For all intents and purposes, he looked the part of a successful businessman. He was well dressed and well spoken! Looking back, I find it comical that I had spent a large proportion of my life up until then, refusing to acknowledge, publicly, my father's illness. However, in that moment, facing the barrel of a gun, I had never been more desperate for the world to acknowledge that he was a sick man.

Many people have asked me where I found the courage to speak out about my dad, in the face of the entire stigma around mental health. For me, it has been a process, and it has been neither easy nor comfortable. The key to my freedom has been to get emotional closure, from pain resulting from past experiences.

Sometimes, you must give yourself what you wish you had gotten from someone else. It took a while; it took a process. Even presently, I occasionally stumble, but I remind myself that I must get up, look up, and keep going. You see, the pain of what happens to you is inevitable, but continuing to suffer, is optional.

So, I began to write, and it is in writing that I found my voice. The story of my life is not finished; it is a puzzle that is still being put together. Writing about my life has allowed me to confront just one of those puzzle pieces. I often think I wish I knew then, what I know now. The fact is that our lives are much more than the memories of our experiences and that maybe all that is required, is the ability to embrace ourselves.

Trusting me

I was in the middle of an exciting work project when I got a call telling me that I needed to fly back home quickly, as my father was gravely ill. I was slightly confused. When did mental illness become life threatening, I thought. It turns out that my father was in a "normal" hospital; *whatever 'normal' may be*! He had not been sick or anything, but now they were telling me he was critically ill.

My plane ride home was agonising. Imagine being alone on a plane, isolated, with thoughts of uncertainty and despair, but praying for a miracle anyway. I was told it was *'touch and go.'* I was in a panicky state. Fear gripped me, *the fear that* dad would not hold on; *the fear* that this would be his last breath, *the fear* of darkness, *the fear* of pain, *the fear* of the unknown, *the fear... full stop.*

When I arrived, I was taken straight to the hospital. Although my dad was unconscious, I sensed he knew I was there. I had *willed* him to hold on, I had prayed for him to *hang in there,* until I got to him, and he did.

I had never seen my father look so frail. He looked very ill but in the same vain, peaceful. I remember getting desperate for him to make things right with God. Now, this may not be important to others, but it was important to me. I prayed with him and asked if he could give me a sign to show that he had heard me. I saw the slightest of smiles, and this gave me hope. I guess this was his way of saying *"it's okay chick"*!

I remember looking around the room and being slightly aware of one of my dad's sisters, huddled in a corner. She was rocking back and forth, holding the largest *prayer beads* I had ever seen in my life! I do not know why, but this memory has forever been imprinted in my mind, whenever I remember this time of my life. Despite the sadness, this picture of my overweight aunt, in the corner of the hospital room, rocking back and forth, often *cracks me up*!

See you later

I had only been with him for a few hours when his breathing changed, it became slightly laboured. In one moment, I saw him breathe in... I waited, and I waited! I remember feeling a sense of panic that he would suffocate if he did not exhale... the next breath never came.

God tapped me on the shoulders that night, and said, *"pardon me"*. Eternity interrupted time and said, "excuse me, this one's mine"! Just like that, my father stepped from this side of time, into the next. And immediately, *'they'* moved from referring to him as, *"he"*, to referring to him as, *"the body"*.

Someone switched off the lights in my world, that day, my heart broke. It was as if somebody had pulled it out of my chest cavity, stomped on it, and tossed it out the window! I wanted to cry, I wanted to scream, I wanted to punch somebody. To me, the question was about what had just happened, at that moment. The whole *thing* was not right, it could not be fair, '*really, God*'?

My Dad died, this is my "tagline" when people ask me about him. It sums up all the information they need. But, for me, it carries a greater reality of what I felt, that day. And it changed me in a way. There was a hole that would never be filled, and I knew I would never be the same. My Dad took a piece of me with him, a piece that will never return. I am incomplete without it; I am incomplete without him.

I have learnt that it does not matter how badly your heart is broken, the world does not stop for your grief. How can it? The world is incapable of stopping, no matter how badly it wants to.

For Real?

Mental illness does not kill. So, what happened in that hospital bed, in that moment, was beyond me.

Towards the end of his life, some of my father family moved in with him. These are the very people who had hounded my mother out of her marriage.

They had made a lot of noise about being better 'supporters' and carers for my father. My father was too soft for his own good. We talked about this at length, and this was probably the only topic that made us mad at each other.

It turns out my father, on one occasion, had a mental health crisis, and one of my cousins beat him up because he did not like the way my dad was behaving. Lesson number one: if you do not like how someone is behaving in his or her own home, you move out! You cannot put your *grubby hands* on a frail old man!

It later became known that this was not the only time my cousin had done this, except on this occasion, he beat my father so badly that his ribs cracked and perforated his lungs, causing him to drown in his own blood!

The thing is that, I know he was fighting *mental illness*, I know he was getting worse as he grew older; I know he was imperfect, but he was mine, and I loved him with all his imperfections!

Some of the family members knew that this abuse was happening but they covered it. I will never understand whether it was out of the fear of *facing* the *ugly truth,* or whether they just did not care. I took it that they just did not care because if you love someone, in my world, you do not bury your head in the sand... you stand up, face the 'ugly,' and you fight!

As if this was not enough, they took advantage of our pain, or confusion, and swindled us out of our inheritance. There were many lies told and a lot of money exchanged to bury the truth. But, I was coming for them! I did not plan what I did that day, it just happened, and when it did, I said enough is enough!

Get unstuck!

Families sometimes look polished on the outside. From an external perspective, we can be impressed and attracted to the cars, homes, or even kids. Behind closed doors, however, family can be hard work. I suspect that every family is to a certain degree, dysfunctional. But, the distinction is not how dysfunctional they are, but how committed the family is to making *things* work.

As for my family and me? How do we continue with the message about how good God is, in the face of such tragedy? I have come to understand that the goodness of God is all around us, always. I guess we only start to question God's goodness when something bad happens. When you think about it, in the face of a great challenge and pain, you can choose to get rid of God. Nevertheless, if you did, would that get rid of your challenge? I believe the scenario remains the same.

It took me years to come to a place of peace, after years of pain and anger. Anger is a poison, which after brewing over, turns to bitterness, and bitterness then distorts your personality, and changes your 'name.'

My heart is on the mend now while other places are still tender, but that is okay because healing is a process. I refuse to let the pain of my past stop me from stepping into my future.

I am learning to forgive, not because I necessarily want to mend relationships, I just want to be free, because unforgiveness can glue you to your past.

My dad died too early in my life, I think, but then, I am not God. I know this for sure, however, that my father loved the Lord and the Lord loved him. In some unknown way, God determined that it was time for my father to go. Most of us have lost someone dear to us. The encouragement I took away from this painful experience was that I had to believe that God knew what he was doing, however ugly the situation was to me.

Sometimes it is hard to trust God when He is not doing what we want Him to be doing. I now have, in hindsight, enough history with him to know what He can do, even though He might not choose to do it. To shift from *parking* in my pain, I have learnt to weigh the bad experience with that history.

The ability to see all the good things He had previously done for me helped me look at my present challenge with eyes of hope; the *hope* that all things would out work themselves for my good, even this mess!

I do not for a moment, believe that God caused my father to die the way he did. I had to be okay with believing and trusting God in faith, for something I will never fully understand but which He himself controls entirely – Death. The pain would gradually ease, but you never forget. I learnt to adopt a position of faith in my circumstance of pain.

Having a history with God will remind us of all the times He has come through for us. This allows us to walk in faith, believing that things will work out for good, no matter what we may be facing at any given time. It allows us to be confident, even when He appears not to come through because in view of the history we have with him, we know He can, and He will. We know that He is good, that He loves us, but we also have to be fully alive to the fact that He is sovereign.

One Step

The only way to experience happiness is to take the responsibility for creating it. You are not responsible for what happened to you in the past, but you are responsible for your attitude now. Why let someone who hurt you in the past, have power over your present? I have also learnt that you can have a sad story in your past, but never build your present, around it.

Pain will keep you trapped in the past thereby causing you to constantly replay an old *record*. At times, the thought of freeing myself through forgiveness, felt as if it was a betrayal to my dad's memory.

I have learnt, however, that reliving the past is detrimental to your present, and that it can also be addictive. In other words, it makes you torture yourself through how you think you could have acted or responded better in that situation

You must remember, regardless of what you could have done, you cannot do it now; it is in the past. I learnt to fight the urge to relive the pain; I cannot not go back into the past and find happiness there. I decided to change the story I was telling myself.

There is no guarantee that you will be able to communicate how you feel to the person who hurt you, and if you can, there is no guarantee they will respond how you want them to. For me, my family lived, and to an extent still do, as if the way my father died, never really happened. It felt as though my father's life did not matter!

It was obvious; I could not find happiness whilst holding onto a painful story. To find my peace, I had to go past what, *'I will never get over'*. I will never get over how my father died, as this is not something you can. You can however get past the pain of the *'what if's'*, and the, *'how could they'?* You must decide to jump from this cycle of pain.

It is not easy to release a *'pain identity,'* particularly if you have carried it around for a long time. It may help to remember who you were, before that experience—or to consider who you might have become if it had not happened. You can still be that person, someone who does not feel bitter or angry, frequently. Make peace with your past, because no matter what you do, it is too late to change it. Forgive those that have hurt you, let go of the old resentments and hurts.

My father would have been proud of who I have become. I hold no resentment. I have a good relationship with some of my father's family because sometimes forgiveness demands that this happens. *It is what it is.*

I write this in memory of my dad. He was more than a man with a tag of mental illness. My dad was an intelligent, funny, hard-working kind and generous individual. If I were to choose a dad all over again, even with what I know now, I would still choose him.

I believe my father is in a better place; I believe in the sovereignty of God and because I believe, I can forgive.